BRIEF
PASTORAL
COUNSELING

BRIEF PASTORAL COUNSELING

Howard W. Stone

Fortress Press

Minneapolis

For Elizabeth and Caitlin Po

BRIEF PASTORAL COUNSELING
Short-term Approach and Strategies

Copyright © 1994 Augsburg Fortress. All rights reserved. Except for brief quotations in critical articles or reviews, no part of this book may be reproduced in any manner without prior written permission from the publisher. Write to: Permissions, Augsburg Fortress, 426 S. Fifth St., Box 1209, Minneapolis MN 55440.

Scripture quotations unless otherwise noted are from the New Revised Standard Version of the Bible, copyright © 1989 by the Division of Christian Education of the National Council of the Churches of Christ in the United States.

Interior design: Linda Crittenden
Cover design: Terry W. Bentley
Cover art: Brad D. Norr

Library of Congress Cataloging-in-Publication Data
Stone, Howard W.
   Brief pastoral counseling : short-term approach and strategies /
Howard W. Stone.
      p.   cm.
   Includes bibliographical references.
   ISBN 0-8006-2720-2 (alk. paper) :
   1. Pastoral counseling. 2. Short-term counseling—Religious
aspects—Christianity.   I. Title.
BV4012.2.S74 1994
253.5—dc20   93-28167
                                          CIP

The paper used in this publication meets the minimum requirements of American National Standard for Information Sciences—Permanence of paper for Printed Library Materials, ANSI Z329, 48-1984. ∞™

Manufactured in the U.S.A.   AF 1-2720

13   14

Contents

Preface

This is a book that I never planned on writing. One evening I was having dinner with a friend, Tim Staveteig, an acquisitions editor at Fortress Press. He asked about the courses I was teaching that semester. We discussed an introductory course on the methods of pastoral counseling, and I mentioned that one of the biggest problems I face in teaching it is that books that would be suitable as texts have been written from the perspective of private practice therapists who tend to have a long-term orientation to their work. This orientation serves a very important function in counseling severely disturbed individuals, but it stands in sharp contrast to the situation of most of my students. They already serve as ministers in churches and most of their counseling consists of a single visit or only a few sessions. Much of their work, in fact, is not only brief but slips in the cracks somewhere between a pastoral care visit and a formal counseling session.

Tim and I discussed some recent research studies which point out that most counseling is brief. (This is true not only for ministers, but also for mental health professionals.)

For me the challenge in teaching an introductory course in pastoral counseling is to guide students in ways of helping parishioners in the few sessions that they have available. Many have already read counseling books written from a long-term perspective.

I asked Tim if he knew of a book that could fit the bill—perhaps one that Fortress Press would be publishing. He knew of no such book. As we completed our meal Tim said, "Howard, I think *you* should write the book on brief pastoral counseling." I immediately declined because of other writing projects and a couple of new courses I was developing, not to mention my desire to spend more time with my family, which included a couple of newish granddaughters (to whom this book is dedicated). But Tim is persistent, and over the next hour he continued to discuss the project. By the time the meal was paid for we had a tentative outline for the book and I had agreed to try and write it.

The majority of the counseling that all ministers (not just students in first parishes) perform is brief. ("Brief" in this book will refer to less than ten sessions. Most counseling offered by pastors is considerably less than ten sessions—typically one to three.) *Brief Pastoral Counseling* proposes an orientation toward pastoral counseling based upon short-term counseling methodology. It assumes that the vast majority of counselees want to deal expeditiously with their problems, because most are unable or unwilling to devote more than a few visits to the task. As Milton Erickson points out, those who come for help seek it "not primarily for enlightenment about the unchangeable past but because of dissatisfaction with the present and a desire to better the future" (Watzlawick et al. 1974, ix). They are seeking help from religious professionals, wanting promptly to address what is troubling them.

The Introduction and Part One of this book present the brief pastoral counseling orientation. These chapters examine in general the methods of brief counseling and discuss how it differs from long-term methods, such as pastoral psychotherapy, that have profoundly influenced pastoral ministry since the middle of the twentieth century. Chapter 1 describes the key characteristics of brief pastoral counseling. Chapter 2 addresses the practice of assigning homework tasks to counselees to do between sessions. Chapter 3 presents a model of problem management that is the basis for the methods of brief pastoral counseling presented in the book.

Part two introduces a series of pastoral counseling interventions. To intervene (from the Latin *intervenire*) means "to come in" or "to come between." In pastoral counseling an intervention is a technique or procedure used to *come between* individuals' existing behaviors and perceptions of reality and their future, desirable ways of doing things or viewing reality. In other words, an intervention is a maneuver used by the helper to bring about the changes which counselees desire.

Interventions take many forms, but all are ways to bring about change through the counseling process. All of the interventions presented in the second section can be used in brief pastoral counseling. Some have been designed specifically for short-term counseling. Others have been borrowed from long-term counseling practice, marriage and family counseling, or from the field of spiritual direction, and adapted for brief pastoral counseling.

PREFACE

Over the past three years my research has been assisted by grants from Brite Divinity School, Texas Christian University, the Evangelical Lutheran Church in America, and the Association for Theological Schools. For all of their help I am grateful.

Much of this book was written during a research leave from 1992 to 1993. The burden of my teaching and supervising responsibility during this time fell to my colleagues at Brite Divinity School, especially Andrew Lester and Nancy Gorsuch, and I am grateful to them for carrying the extra load. In addition, I want to thank the ministers and counselors in this country and in England who allowed me the opportunity to discuss with them how they do short-term counseling. I also am indebted to the many persons who have helped in the writing effort, especially those who read all or portions of the manuscript: Howard Clinebell, Timothy Dice, and Joey Jeter. Finally I want to express my deep gratitude to Karen Stone who gave many hours of her time in reviewing the text.

Many of the ideas presented in this book are drawn from my day-to-day practice of pastoral care and counseling. Consequently the book contains elements of actual case histories. Since confidentiality is essential to pastoral practice, all case descriptions have been altered with respect to names and other identifiers in order to preserve anonymity while not distorting the essential reality of the experience described.

Introduction

The Case for Brief
Pastoral Counseling

In an early scene of Woody Allen's *Annie Hall*, the character Max stands outside Annie Hall's apartment building making awkward small talk with his new acquaintance. Annie invites him up for a glass of wine, adding in her self-depreciating way that he doesn't have to because he's probably late for something. Max says he'd like that very much. "I've got time. I've got nothing till my analyst appointment."

"Oh," she says. "Well, you see an analyst?"

"Ah . . . yeah . . . [diffidently] just for fifteen years."

"Fifteen years?!" Annie exclaims.

Max looks embarrassed. "Yeah. I'm going to give him one more year, and then I'm gonna go to Lourdes."

How much time will people give a minister or pastoral counselor to effect change in their situations before going to Lourdes? Or giving up? Or calling it "good enough" and getting on with their lives? Not sixteen years. Not sixteen months. Rarely even sixteen counseling sessions.

Some people do enter long-term counseling relationships and spend years in analysis—quite possibly even when little change is discernable in their daily lives. Characters like Max have become media stereotypes of people who seek professional help for their problems. But in fact such long-standing, doggedly faithful counselees are *not* typical.

Over the past two decades I have become increasingly interested in knowing more about the people who come to a minister or pastoral counselor for counseling. While many questions could be raised concerning the nature of the pastor-counselee relationship, the theological reflections on that relationship, and the necessary intervention methods, my questions have been more direct: Who are these persons? What do they really want from a minister or counselor? What beliefs do they bring to the relationship? What hopes do they hold out for its outcome? Do they really want to change?

I am not alone in my questioning. Most ministers and counselors have considerable opportunity to reflect on these questions. One indicator of what people *want* in counseling is what they end up *doing* or not doing. The fact is that after the first session, most people do not return for many additional sessions, so the pastoral counseling process is typically a short one. In addition to relief from their distress or solutions to their problems, *what people also want from counseling is that it be brief.*

Is this a sign of the times? In our fast food, instant coffee, sixty minute photo developing, crash diet, microwave-in-a-minute age, have people lost their patience to work toward long-term solutions to their problems? Is the desire for a "quick fix" part of their pathology? Or is it a sign of health, of a willingness to tackle a problem head-on and promptly do what is needed to get on with the business of living?

It is impossible to say. Either a desire for an instant solution or a willingness to address situations directly, or both, may be present in any given case. One person may be looking for a bromide or the wave of a magic wand; another may need some advice, a strategy, a way to go about achieving balance or breaking out of a harmful pattern of behavior; another may be financially unable to afford more than a short series of sessions with a therapist in private practice; and others may be between jobs, or expect to leave the area shortly, and so on.

Whatever the motivation, the fact remains that a minister spends on average only two or three hours counseling most parishioners or family units; many counseling encounters are limited to a single session. Even people who have agreed to longer counseling often stop coming after a few sessions.

The short-term nature of pastoral counseling may cause some ministers to undervalue their work. A common misperception is that brief counseling methods are inferior to long-term approaches (Sifneos 1972, x-xi; Phillips and Wiener 1966, 2). Short-term approaches are regarded as the best methods when working with people who are poor, people who are not insight-oriented, undereducated persons, those who cannot delay gratification, and some minority groups. Long-term counseling, in contrast, is often described as depth counseling, insight-oriented, dynamic, and intensive—the therapy that gets to the root of a problem and yields enduring benefits. Sifneos (1972, x) describes the entrenched attitude that long-term therapy is superior, stating that it considers the helper indispensable to counselees and

> has been responsible, by and large, for the resistance encountered by those who have tried to shorten the length of psychotherapy and for the prevailing confusion about the use of the terms "brief," "crisis oriented," and "short-term psychotherapy." Although the short-term interview is the only element which a variety of therapeutic techniques have in common with each other, they are usually considered to be identical and are largely ignored.

Brief Pastoral Counseling proposes that most people in counseling do not require long-term methods and indeed that short-term methods will be equally as effective. In spite of this, long-term counseling still has a significant place and benefit. Some people will not be helped by brief counseling and yet others will not be helped by either short-term or long-term care. (See the conclusion for situations where referral to long-term psychotherapy may be better than brief pastoral counseling.) *Brief Pastoral Counseling* addresses not so much an ideal method of counseling by helpers as it does the method of counseling actually practiced. The startling conclusion reached by researchers in recent years across the various mental health disciplines is that the majority of counseling performed today is short-term. (The details of several studies supporting this contention are summarized in notes at the end of this introduction.)[1]

The difficulty is that while most counseling is primarily short-term, many therapists have been taught—and continue to believe—that long-term therapy is the preferable and more desirable approach.

Clergy seem to share this prejudice with other professionals. Many believe in the superiority of long-term methods, but for a variety of practical reasons rarely engage in long-term counseling. As a result, numerous ministers believe they are offering second class care.

The aim of *Brief Pastoral Counseling* is not to persuade ministers to practice short-term counseling. Like mental health professionals, ministers already are engaged in a brief number of sessions with counselees. Rather, *Brief Pastoral Counseling* addresses the dissonance

3

that occurs when one believes in the superiority of long-term counseling, but engages primarily in short-term care. This book presents an orientation to brief pastoral counseling and suggests some methods of doing it. Those interested in more detailed discussions of the efficacy of brief counseling methods compared to long-term counseling are urged to study the works of Childs (1990), de Shazer (1985; 1988; 1991), Haley (1973; 1976), Sifneos (1972), and Wells (1982). The remainder of *Brief Pastoral Counseling* is based on these documented studies of the value of brief counseling.

UNDERLYING CAUSES OF PROBLEMS

Salvador Minuchin, a pioneer in systems therapy, received the following letter from a struggling parent who was a complete stranger to him (1988, 90):

Dear Dr. Minuchin:
I have a daughter who is an anorexic. She is 5'3" and weighs 80 pounds. The condition was diagnosed a year ago, and she has been hospitalized twice when her weight went below the minimum set by the attending physician. She has been in therapy ever since, but stays pretty much the same. It's creating problems for the whole family; she makes lavish desserts that she insists everybody else has to eat, she drinks all the fruit juice in the refrigerator, hides containers of vomit around the house, and in general, lies about anything and everything connected with her consumption of food and drink.
She is obsessed with exercise and what to eat, when to eat, etc. We do not believe we make any excessive demands on her; in fact, rather the opposite. She is an overachiever, third in her class.
I asked the doctor last week if he felt that she has made any improvement, and his comment was definitely yes, but that it may take one to ten years to straighten everything out. I brought up the subject of behavioral therapy, which I know is quick, but he said it would only remove the anorexia, and if you remove one problem another will surface in its place. He prefers to get to the bottom, the origin, no matter how long that takes.
I feel that if you remove the most harmful problems first, although the underlying one will still be there, certain other pieces of the puzzle might fall into place. At this stage of the game I am totally confused. I am appealing to you. We need help desperately, both for my daughter's health and for the sake of our family.

Many of us who grew up under the shadow of Freud have assumed that dealing with a problem effectively means getting at its roots. In this school of thought, any difficulty requiring serious attention should be entrusted to an expert who can dig out its underlying causes. The "problem" is only a symptom; something deeper lurks behind it, and one's past needs to be explored to get to the problem's fundamental causes. The letter to Minuchin portrays these assumptions and their painful consequences. The parents' agony can be felt as they search for a more expeditious solution before the physical and emotional damage to their daughter becomes too great. They are trapped by a particular way of thinking that is applied to many issues in today's society: the way to help convicted criminals is to analyze what led them to their behavior; the way to deal with child abusers is to examine their upbringing; and so forth.

On the surface, such a theory makes sense, but two things work against the assumption that getting at the roots of a problem is the best or only means of relieving it. First, in practice, extensive exploration of a person's history is *not* necessary for effective change; finding the sources of a problem often is not a prerequisite for change. An individual's history should not be glossed over or neglected, however, but in most cases extensive time given to such exploration is not a condition for positive change.

Second, when people begin to understand some of the underlying causes of their problems, resolutions do not automatically follow. Even profound insight frequently proves insufficient; it supplies rich data for reflection and maturation, but does not necessarily lead to the specific change that originally motivated the person to seek care. Haley (1976) writes that helping counselees understand themselves has nothing to do with helping them change; most therapists make people more self-aware but do not make them aware of their potential.

Focusing on a problem's causes often leads to a criticism of short-term counseling methods. Counselors often believe that because short-term methods do not get to the underlying roots of a problem, any changes that occur will not endure. This thinking is understandable. Crash diets, for instance, tend to result in eventual weight gain. A hurry-up job of housecleaning will soon need to be done again. Hasty conclusions are often wrong. This way of thinking, however, is not validated by research.

Several studies have looked at the durability of change in brief counseling by including follow-up assessment methods in their research design (Fisher 1980, 1984; Langsley et al. 1971; Reid and Shyne

1969; Sloane et al. 1975; Wells et al. 1977). Follow-up evaluations in these studies took place from four months to two and one-half years after the completion of counseling. The findings of these studies are surprisingly consistent. Although some minor deterioration of counseling results was noted at the time of follow up for short-term counseling, its deterioration is no different than that suffered by any other psychotherapeutic modality—long-term included. The durability of benefits from brief counseling methods are equal to those of long-term therapy. Consequently, ministers do not need to feel that they are somehow shortchanging their parishioners by offering them brief care.

BRIEF AND LONG-TERM COUNSELING COMPARED

What about the character of change in brief counseling? It would seem that with less time available, counseling goals would be more difficult to realize. Outcome studies of counseling are difficult to interpret because of the near impossibility for any two researchers or theoreticians to agree even upon a definition of a good counseling outcome. Nevertheless, these studies at least provide a sense of the effect of time upon counseling results. In spite of differing methods, controls, and criteria, not one of these outcome studies found any correlation between length of therapy and degree of improvement. All studies found that short-term methods were at least as effective as long-term methods, and that the only significant difference was the length of time required for the changes to occur.[2]

How can these and similar studies best be interpreted? Even though they are not conclusive, the assumption that long-term counseling methods are superior to short-term methods is not confirmed and seems to be incorrect. Granted, the American Psychological Association's Task Force on Health Research has claimed that more contact with an individual in counseling means a greater chance that long-term benefits will result, but the only research that justifies this claim is an unpublished work on encouraging toothbrushing (Janis 1983, 56). Outcome studies also indicate that considerable benefits are gained in very short periods of time. As early as 1962, Phillips and Wiener (1962, 21) concluded their review of a number of outcome studies on short- and long-term counseling by stating, "Long-termness or interminability of treatment seems most likely to be determined by the dependency and the conceptual needs of the patient and by the personality and theory of the therapist, and it apparently has little direct relationship to improvement in treatment."

BRIEF COUNSELING: THE MINISTER'S FIRST CHOICE

The viewpoint presented in this book is that brief pastoral counseling methods, for most people encountered in the parish, are not only as good as longer methods but are actually better because they take less time and are equally effective. This fact alone suggests that brief methods should be the approach of first choice for clergy in congregational settings.

The first choice, however, does not mean the only choice. The studies that compare brief and long-term counseling are clear: Short-term therapy helps individuals reach their counseling goals as much as extended care. Long-term methods, however, need not be entirely abandoned by the pastoral counselor. Short-term pastoral counseling should be offered to persons who do not require long-term care; a majority of those who seek help from clergy do not need or want long-term care.

What accounts for a similarity in outcomes of brief and long-term methods? Meltzoff and Kornreich (1970, 357) extensively reviewed outcome studies as they reviewed existing therapeutic modalities and concluded that successful counseling achieves its major gains earlier in the counseling process. A *window of opportunity* seems present early in a helping relationship when people are more open to making changes in their lives. The majority of change, when it occurs, happens in the first few counseling sessions.

Additional reasons make brief pastoral counseling methods the best choice for use with most individuals in the parish. First, one of the difficulties with long-term methods is that most people who initiate counseling (regardless of what they have agreed to do) only come for a few sessions and never finish. (This is perhaps the best-kept secret in the counseling profession.) Individuals engaged in short-term care are more apt to make at least a few changes that can begin resolving their problems before they drop out. In contrast, people in long-term therapy who drop out usually do so while they are still in the process of uncovering the roots of their problems and have not yet begun to make positive changes. As Wells (1982, 5) writes:

> Whatever the modality of intervention, many clients do not stay in treatment if emphasis is placed on such broad concepts as personality

7

reorganization or overall personal growth in the context of long-term contact. Where systematic studies have been conducted, it has been found that mental health clinics and family service agencies have appallingly high drop-out rates. Access to many clients is comparatively brief, and the *carer must be prepared to work in the most helpful manner possible within these limitations rather than futilely wish that there was more time.* (italics mine)

If the carer can expect to dedicate one to three sessions in a typical parish pastoral counseling relationship (which is much briefer than what many early theorists established as short-term), the care must be structured around one to three sessions rather than around some ideal that presumes an unlimited number of sessions. In brief pastoral counseling, each session should be regarded as potentially the last one. At each meeting, every effort should be made to provide counselees with what they require in order to resolve their distress. For whatever reason, they may never return, and therefore they should be provided with what they need to carry on.

Efficiency is another reason for using short-term methods as a first approach in parish counseling. The studies cited suggest that brief counseling methods help resolve people's problems faster than open-ended counseling. This more closely accommodates the desires of most counselees—rapidly resolving their troubles. Most people seeking help do not want to commit long periods of time to therapy; they are unwilling to pay the price either in money or time. I do not advocate rushing the caregiving process, but a brief form of counseling is by its brevity more desirable than an equally effective process that is more time consuming.

A third benefit of using brief pastoral counseling methods is that they are better adapted to ministers' other responsibilities. The time that can be given to counseling, when weighed against the other tasks of parish ministry, is limited. As a result, clergy practicing short-term pastoral counseling are able to offer help to a greater number of individuals. This helps to resolve the moral dilemma that faces many pastors: balancing the quality of care with the immensity of need. Short-term methods are compatible with pastoral care visitation and with informal pastoral encounters that fall somewhere between pastoral care visitation and a more formal pastoral counseling session. A number of the interventions presented in this book lend themselves to making this transition between pastoral care and formal pastoral counseling, something that needs to be done with some regularity in parish ministry.

Until recently (with the exception of crisis intervention), neither pastoral counseling nor psychotherapy has generated much interest in the development of strategies for shortening the counseling process. Instead, the focus often has been on engaging counselees in the therapeutic process so that they will stay for longer periods of time. If counselees did not persist they were considered "not motivated enough."[3]

Few people—unlike Woody Allen's Max—have the time, the need, or the perseverance required of extended periods of treatment. This book provides a methodology of brief pastoral counseling that applies to a broader range of situations than crisis counseling alone, befits the congregational setting, and shortens the process of pastoral counseling while it preserves or even enhances the quality of care given.

Notes to the Introduction

1. Beck and Jones (1973) examined 3,596 cases in family service agencies across the United States for the length of time persons were in counseling. They compared their results to a similar survey in 1960 and discovered a significant shift toward brief counseling. Indeed, in their research, short-term cases averaged five sessions, but even "continued service" cases, which the agencies would consider long-term, averaged only nine visits.

In a more recent study, Langsley (1978) examined 4,072 psychiatric cases seen in both clinics and private practice. It might be expected that psychiatrists would see individuals for considerably longer periods than would other mental health or helping professionals, yet the median number of visits to private practitioners was 12.8, and only 10.3 for clinic psychiatrists. How remarkably brief for psychiatric care!

In another study of counseling that took place in an outpatient clinic, Garfield and Kurtz (1977) reported similar results. They considered 1,216 cases and found the average number of sessions to be six, with very few individuals seen for more than ten visits. In fact, they noted that 57.7 percent of the counseling was completed in one to four sessions.

Phillips (1985) reviewed student visits to a university counseling center over a four year period. He found that about one-half of the students did not return for a second visit. Thus one-half of all counseling cases were of the one session variety. Bloom (Phillips 1985) investigated whether those who did not return for more than one session were dissatisfied with counseling. He discovered the contrary, that two-thirds reported "satisfaction" with the counseling but did not return because they either no longer felt a need or, due to practical changes in their lives, felt some sense of resolution.

2. Stieper and Wiener (Phillips and Wiener 1962, 21) divided clients into long- and short-term counseling groups, controlling for education, intelligence, and diagnosis. Their work identified no correlation between the time spent in therapy and the degree of improvement:

> The great majority of long-term patients were being seen by a small minority of the therapists. A likely reason appears to be failure on the part of "long-term" therapists adequately to formulate therapy goals and to personalize the therapeutic relationship.

Another study reported by Garetz, Kogl, and Wiener (1959), using a somewhat different research methodology also failed to find superior improvement among long-term therapy clients.

INTRODUCTION

Time-limited therapy, a form of short-term therapy in which the counselor sets specific limits with the counselee on how much time will be devoted to the counseling process (e.g., four sessions, or three weeks, or "by December 15"), was the focus of a study comparing Rogerian client-centered and Adlerian approaches (Phillips and Wiener 1962, 55–56). The study reported that those who received time-limited therapy and those given unlimited time therapy, regardless of the therapeutic approach, showed equal improvement. The only difference noted between the two groups was that the gains achieved by the time-limited group occurred in about one-half as many counseling sessions.

Munch (Phillips and Wiener 1962, 135) compared long-term, short-term, and time-limited therapeutic results over a five year period. The study included 105 individuals divided equally among the three groups. Short-term was considered three to seven sessions, time-limited eight to nineteen sessions, and long-term as twenty or more sessions with no arbitrary termination. The author chose these numbers because previous research had indicated a "failure zone" somewhere between the twelfth and twenty-first interview, and it was believed that shortening the span of counseling might discourage its development. The results suggested that significant positive counseling benefits accrued for short-term and time-limited therapy clients, but not for those in long-term care.

Reid and Shyne (1969) randomly assigned 120 cases, predominantly marriage and family issues, to either brief counseling (eight sessions or less) or unlimited counseling. Through a variety of assessment measures, they discovered that a short-term approach was at least as effective as a long-term approach, and in some categories more effective.

Beck and Jones (1973) reviewed over three thousand cases of counseling that involved a mixture of marital, family, and personal problems. Their study indicated that brief counseling methods were equally or slightly more effective than long-term methods. Leventhal and Weinberger (1975), in a study of over one thousand cases, came up with the same results: short-term counseling was as or more effective than long-term counseling.

A study by Sloane and his colleagues (1975) compared the results of psychodynamic and behavioral short-term counseling with a control group who received no treatment. Evaluation of the counseling was extensive and carried out by the counselor, client, family members, and an independent psychotherapist who did not participate in the care. Substantial improvement was found in both treatment groups as compared to those who received no treatment. No differences in effectiveness were found between the two psychotherapeutic modalities.

Other studies with similar results include those by Frank (1979), Garfield (1980), Luborsky and others (1975), Strupp (1978), and Wells (1982).

3. Clergy who do a significant amount of counseling rely upon works in the fields of psychotherapy and pastoral counseling for resource material which, for the most part, are biased toward the superiority of long-term

methods. The majority are based on theoretical constructs and psychotherapeutic modalities of long-term counseling, even when written for helpers in the parish setting who usually see individuals for only a few sessions.

Part One

---

*THE
SHORT-TERM
STRATEGY*

1
Resolving Problems

How should counseling be approached? Quick and dirty? Short and sweet? Or skillful and exact? It is a mistake to assume that the shorter the counseling approach, the easier its performance or the less sophisticated its technique. In fact, considerable pastoral artistry is needed to translate a parishioner's vague uneasiness into a specific problem, focus on the key issues, and motivate her or him toward bringing about the needed change—all within a short time. Inertia in both helper and helpee works against all but a sophisticated approach.

THE CASE OF ROGER PENDLEY

Pastor Christine Lin made a routine visit to the Pendley household on one bright spring afternoon. The Pendleys' two high school daughters had come home only minutes before the pastor's visit, and the house was in a general uproar. The refrigerator was under search-and-seizure, and the events of the day were described in bursts of lively detail.

After a few minutes, when the daughters had vanished to their rooms, Pastor Lin was alone with Gloria Pendley, who served as the church school superintendent. They were working out the last few details for a summer education program.

About nine months earlier, Gloria's 71-year-old father-in-law, Roger, had come to live with them. He had joined the household for several reasons: to get away from the cold and the rising taxes in New York; to leave his changing and increasingly violent neighborhood; to cope with the first signs of cataracts; and to appease his son's increasing concern about his well-being. The most significant reason for the move, though, was his limited income. Roger Pendley had worked as a machinist all his life, and four union officials had absconded with most of the company's pension funds, leaving Roger with nothing but his Social Security checks.

When Pastor Lin asked Gloria how her father-in-law was doing, she rolled her eyes and replied, "Why don't you ask *him*?" The two had talked about the elder Mr. Pendley and his difficulties before, but this was the first hint of exasperation on her part.

To avoid intruding on the family, Roger Pendley often spent most of each day in his room on the lower level of the house. Pastor Lin knocked on his door and exchanged a few pleasantries with him. On this particular day she thought that he was rather withdrawn. He reminisced about his old home and the shop in his basement "back East." Clearly he was feeling useless and in the way. He could no longer be productive and, with his cataracts, even reading and watching television were difficult. Roger cloistered himself in his room, but when he joined the family, he admitted giving too much advice to his son and daughter-in-law about the raising of their children, which only caused greater strain.

How might one respond to Roger Pendley? Is counseling necessary? Several responses seem possible in such a situation.

■ One response would be not to act, assuming that Roger would adapt to his new life over time. Although this would have been a viable response earlier, his struggles have not abated nine months after moving and in fact have intensified.

■ A second response might be to make several additional pastoral visits to *his* home, that is, coming to see Roger. Such an approach has merit and an informal sort of counseling might occur.

■ A third option might include crisis intervention methods. They might have been useful for Mr. Pendley when he first arrived at his son's home, but he is no longer in a crisis state and those methods are less appropriate now (see Stone 1993). Mr. Pendley is living with the fallout of the earlier crisis.

■ A fourth response would be to recommend family counseling to the three generations of Pendleys. Such an approach makes Roger Pendley's problem everyone's problem and not his alone—it involves the whole family. (In fact, in the actual case described here the family did become involved to some extent.)

■ Extended psychotherapy, or pastoral psychotherapy, is another option. It was not chosen because it appeared that the problem could be addressed in a brief time. The rule of parsimony, applied to care situations, suggests that less is more. If the difficulty can be handled competently in a few sessions, then using a greater number of sessions is wasteful.

THE TIME FACTOR

Timing and time are important factors throughout the counseling process. When people come for counseling, it is critical to explore the reasons that prompted them to come when they did or what prevented them from realizing that their problems needed to be addressed. Likewise, structuring a "family intervention" for an alcoholic member is a matter of good timing; it is crucial to determine the best day and hour for the confrontation to occur. To a significant degree, timing sets the immediate context for responding to others.

Time is equally important to those who seek counsel because it regulates access and outcomes. Specifically mentioning a time limitation is important in pastoral care and counseling because a pastor's other demands leave a limited time for counseling. The minister's role seldom allows additional time for counseling parishioners without impinging on other responsibilities. If the helper does not have more than thirty minutes to give, it is best to let the counselees know at the beginning of the session.

Time is also important to those who seek the minister's counsel. Before scheduling an interview, it is good for the minister to answer the following questions: How available am I? Do I set up a time that makes it easy for them to come? Is it difficult for individuals to see me? Do I show up on time for the interview? Am I able to give them the entire period that I promised? People need to know how much of the pastor's time will be theirs; it provides a framework for the counseling process. The time allotted to the counseling process needs to be organized so it is used as efficiently as possible. One method of shortening the counseling process is to structure the counseling for a specific number of sessions.

In the case of Roger Pendley, Pastor Lin might have said: "Since we have decided what the goal in the counseling is to be, I'd like to suggest that we spend three sessions working together on the issues. While we are doing it, you will have to do homework tasks to help address these issues. At the end of the sessions we can review your accomplishments. Certainly, if more needs to be done, then we can structure additional sessions or I can refer you to someone in our community who can continue on with you. How does that sound to you?"

Such structuring, referred to as *time-limited counseling*, generally occurs in the relationship-building or assessment phases of counseling and provides counselees a framework in which to deal with their problems. It adds to brief pastoral counseling the step of arranging a specific number of counseling sessions to address a particular problem; informs individuals from the outset that time is crucial (that only a particular number of sessions will be given to dealing with their problem); and lets individuals know that they need to get down to business, that what happens is serious.

The framework, however, cannot be allowed to overtake the context of concern for the person who requests assistance. Troubled persons should not feel as though they are being rushed out the door. They need rather to sense that their problems are being taken seriously, and that the minister is not at their disposal for an afternoon chat.

One reason for structuring counseling with a limited number of sessions is to encourage persons to focus their time in counseling. People work harder and accomplish more when they know that time is limited (Mann 1973). As E. L. Phillips puts it, "Whenever something appears open-ended as to time, it tends to lull us into inactivity, encourage postponement, wastefulness" (Phillips 1985, 4).

This dynamic of focus and pace became clear to me while participating as a counselee in two therapy groups. The first one began at 7:00 P.M. and continued until the group decided to stop, which was usually between 9:30 and 11:00. The second was limited to one and one-half hours each session, not a minute more. Each group was led by a competent pastoral counselor. Both groups took a few initial sessions to get under way and both accomplished about the same amount therapeutically. The difference was that one did in an hour and a half what the other took three or four hours to accomplish. Although the time limitation in this example was the length of time per session rather than the number of sessions (which was the same for both groups), the effect of limited time was that a group of twelve got to work within a matter of minutes, while the group with unlimited time usually took an hour or so before focusing.

Brief pastoral counseling does *not* require a structured number of sessions. Indeed, I do not often use time-limited counseling except when I work with one of two groups of people: those who are hesitant to commit time and energy to counseling, and those who settle back in counseling with their arms folded, waiting to see what I will do. Counselees, however, need to be made aware through the style of the minister's leadership that time is crucial.

Limiting time—or using any brief counseling method—does not mean taking actions precipitously or neglecting to think through their possible effects. Short-term methods most certainly are not quick and dirty nor do they offer the promise of overnight results which underlies much popular self-help literature. The purpose of limiting the time spent is that once a course of action is decided upon, counselees can move unhesitatingly toward accomplishing their own ends. All short-term counseling schools are termination-determined methods. Whether they apply time constraints, goal achievement, or both, they recognize time limitations and expeditiously structure the counseling from beginning to end.

THE PERSPECTIVE OF
BRIEF PASTORAL COUNSELING

The abbreviated time that most counselees give helpers (and that helpers can structure into the relationship) makes endless sessions of talking without focus a luxury. Instead, the pastoral counseling process must be geared to focus on key issues, develop a plan for change, and help counselees take concrete actions. Brief pastoral counseling is not so much a series of newly developed techniques as an outlook for or *perspective* on pastoral counseling. As an orientation to the pastoral helping process, it forms what is done. It shapes how relations are established, what questions are important, how time is used, what counseling methods are practiced, and how they are employed. Brief pastoral counseling is a particular vision of helping that influences all aspects of the care enterprise.

The major components of the brief counseling perspective follow.

Establish a Brief Counseling Orientation

Even though the majority of all counseling is brief in nature because people stop coming, short-term counseling cannot be defined only by the number of sessions. Rather the *orientation* to the care distinguishes brief pastoral counseling from other approaches. The attitude toward the helping process and the specific interventions employed are more defining than the actual number of sessions.

Brief pastoral counseling uses the least extreme method—the least invasive, simplest approach—in any situation. Resorting to an elaborate approach before knowing whether a counselee will return for further sessions may be a waste of time.

The helper should also avoid presuming that people's problems can be completely solved. Some of the cases discussed in this book are rather complex; they describe counselees with numerous and apparently irresolvable difficulties, enough to make most helpers want to throw up their hands and refer them to someone else. Brief pastoral counseling's goal is not to solve all of an individual's or family's difficulties. Its goal is more modest, and therefore more likely to succeed.

The short-term approach assumes a ripple effect—that a change initiated in one area of an individual's life will generalize and spread to other areas. Erickson states: "That little hole in the dike [does not seem like it will] flood the land, except that it will, because once you break through an altered pattern of behavior in some way, the cracks keep traveling" (Haley 1985, 1:102). Change is contagious. The important thing is to start the change process so that the success of change in one area will spread to others.

A small number of counseling sessions also hinders the formation of dependency relationships in the helping process and encourages counselees to address their problems with their new or renewed resources. Moreover, a smaller number of sessions recognizes finitude; it assumes that we are part of a world caught up in individual and corporate sin, anxiety, losses, doubts, and too many conflicts to mention. Evil is pervasive. Pastoral counseling's task is not to eradicate all of the maladies of sin and evil, but rather to help others *begin* addressing the problems they face and to be faithful to God's call.

Establish an Empathetic Relationship

The crucial first step in counseling, doubly important in brief pastoral counseling, is to establish a solid base of rapport and acceptance with the troubled individual. From the onset of the first session the minister motivates counselees and makes them cooperative with change. This involves physically attending to the other person by listening carefully, temporarily suspending judgment, and offering appropriate warmth and respect. The minister may already have a good relationship with the individual who comes in with a problem, such as with Christine Lin and Roger Pendley. What is required, then, is to strengthen the already existing relationship.

In counseling relationships, pastors earn the right to say certain things or use particular interventions. The helper's role, however, does not automatically convey respect. Most troubled individuals do not take helpers seriously unless they respect them. Respect is gained mostly by establishing caring relationships with counselees—by allowing the troubled person to experience and share his or her feelings. These caring skills (usually termed 'empathic') have been detailed extensively in pastoral care and psychotherapeutic literature (see, for example, Egan 1990; Clinebell 1984; Stone 1991, 1993).

Focus on the Problem

"If therapy is to end properly, it must begin properly—by negotiating a solvable problem" (Haley 1976, 9). One of the first tasks in brief pastoral counseling is to identify the central problem(s). The general issues being presented need to be defined clearly and in specific, concrete terms. They need to be stated in a way that makes them solvable. Describing someone as having low self-esteem, for example, is vague and is not a specific definition of a problem. How would anyone know when a person's self-esteem is successfully elevated?

A more precise definition in Roger Pendley's case might be: "I am depressed. I wanted to leave my home back East, but now I miss the activities and friends I had there. I have been too passive about finding new things to do or making new friends. I have made my family here my only friends, and when I've told them how I feel I have been too 'bossy,' not letting my son and daughter-in-law run their own family in their own way."

The more concrete and specific the definition of the problem, the more readily solutions will be available. It is essential, therefore, from the opening moments of brief pastoral counseling to focus on the key problem(s). The dominant concern in brief pastoral counseling is not basic change in personality, but the management of

21

specific problems. The personality will be modified to some extent, but is not the primary goal.

Assess the Problem

The medical model (diagnosis first, treatment second) is not necessarily the pastoral model. Assessment in brief pastoral counseling does not require all of the facts before one can begin managing the problem. Diagnosis and treatment, assessment and change-oriented activities, occur continuously throughout each session. The process of solving people's problems can begin within minutes after beginning the first interview. Because assessment is an ongoing process, much is learned once counselees begin to act. The focus of assessment in brief pastoral counseling is looking for *cues* (stimuli) that trigger the onset of the problem and the *reinforcers* (rewards) that maintain it.

Assessment is a task in which both pastor and counselee participate and not just what the pastor does for the counselee. Assessment itself is not lengthy, even though the process of assessment is never really completed until the sessions are ended. Extensively exploring a person's history or discerning the underlying causes of behavior is not essential; the counselee does not need insight in order to act.

What happens in each counseling session is much more important than causative explanations of behaviors. Weakland et al. (1974, 145) suggest that no matter what the cause of complaints (if a cause can even be reliably discerned), complaints "persist only if they are maintained by ongoing current behavior of the [person] and others with whom he interacts. Correspondingly, if such problem-maintaining behavior is appropriately changed or eliminated, the problem will be resolved or vanish, regardless of its nature, origin, or duration."

A vital question ministers need to ask counselees is: "Why now?" With all of the problems, stresses, and strains that individuals find themselves under each day, what has led them to counseling at this moment? For example, what prompted a married couple, after twenty-five years of fighting, to request counseling today?

Literally asking counselees "Why now?" sometimes yields an answer, although some individuals need to be asked more than once and in different ways. *The danger for most helpers*—mental health professionals, and ministers alike—is that when a quick response to the question "Why now?" is not heard, they begin addressing obvious character or personality flaws in the counselees. To do so is to move into long-term counseling. In such cases, the goals to be achieved are no longer those of the counselee, but of the helper. This leads to what Budman and Gurman (1988) describe as "total overhaul therapy." Such counseling almost automatically glosses over the strength of counselees and their existing network of supports, and focuses on liabilities. To omit the why–now question is to put aside people's immediate needs and concerns and to attend to predetermined personality reconstruction based upon the helper's own definition of a healthy personality, which is not the task of brief counseling.

"How fast do you want counseling to go?" is another question that sometimes is useful, especially with eager individuals who want the counseling to be finished quickly. Brief counseling done rapidly is as competent and effective as when it is slower, but it will be an exceedingly rigorous experience. The counselor might warn the counselee: "You will have to work extremely hard, and you should only consider doing this if you are desperate enough to go through it." Sometimes it is beneficial to let people consider this option for a few days before they make a decision.

Another important part of the assessment process is to discern counselees' previous attempts at change so that the minister can set aside these options as less workable. Persons often have received advice from other sources, but have been unable to follow it. W. C. Fields' admonition applies to these situations: "If at first you don't succeed, try, try, again. Then give up. There's no use being a damn fool about it." Well-meaning helpers too often offer *more of the same* counseling. If it hasn't worked in the past, don't try it again. Try something unrelated to previous attempts at solutions—perhaps even something opposite.

One quick way to gain information about counselees is to use counseling checklists. Checklists, frequently only a page or two in length, can rapidly give pastors an idea of the breadth of the troubling issues. Since the goals of brief pastoral counseling are modest, many problem areas discovered are not focused on, but checklists help both pastor and counselee to concentrate on the key areas (see Appendix A for an example of a checklist).

Look for Exceptions

People seeking counseling tend to think that their problem exists all of the time. In fact, they do not notice when their problem is absent, or they pass its absence off as an accident. Assessment pays attention not only to cues or reinforcers of problem behaviors but also to what Steve de Shazer calls *exceptions,* which are "whatever is happening when the complaint is not" (1988, 53). Parents may claim that their son "beats up on his sisters all of the time." Whatever the amount of violence he actually inflicts (this should not be over-looked), the son is not literally being violent "all of the time." de Shazer (1991, 58) suggests that

> problems are seen to maintain themselves simply because they maintain themselves and because clients depict the problem as *always happening.* Therefore, times when the complaint is absent are dismissed as trivial by the client or even remain completely unseen, hidden from the client's view. . . . For the client, the problem is seen as primary (and the exceptions, if seen at all, are seen as secondary).

In brief pastoral counseling, the exceptions are of primary importance and may serve as the central focus of the counseling.

Looking for exceptions requires questions other than those cus-tomarily asked in counseling (O'Hanlon and Weiner-Davis 1989), such as: "How different are periods when you are not fighting with your spouse?" "How did you achieve them?" "What are they like?" "Did your spouse, family, or friends notice when you were not fighting?" "How could you tell that they noticed?" and "How did you stop the fighting?"

Another approach is to compliment one or both partners. For example, you might say: "I am impressed you did not get into a fight last weekend when your son took the car without permission." The minister calls attention to the time that they did not get into a fight, thus a time of strength is emphasized rather than the times of difficulty. "I am impressed" is stated in the present tense even if the incident occurred a long time ago. This approach assumes that people are able not to fight or become unduly defensive when provoked.

Homework tasks are often assigned. In the example of a couple that occasionally argues, the homework might be: "Observe in the coming week whatever happens in your relationship with your wife that you want to continue happening." When exceptions to the prob-lem state are discovered, counselees should be urged to do more of what they did. These exceptions then become homework tasks. The task should not suggest something new to counselees, but urge them to do more of something they already do. These exceptions can then become the goal of the counseling.

Establish Limited Goals

Communication theorist Robert Norton (de Shazer 1991, 53) has suggested that while "much of psychiatry spends time trying to unravel the correct, clear cause of the problem with a crystalline analysis devoid of inconsistencies and pure in its structural flow, the brief therapist will settle for a dirty solution that works. The flow of the structure can be marred, illogical, and inconsistent as long as the solution works." Information often inhibits action because it is not focused on acting. O'Hanlon and Weiner-Davis (1989, 38) note that helpers "often get stuck because they have too much information rather that too little, or too much information about the problem and too little about the solution." I have noticed that most beginning pastoral counselors spend more time developing an analysis of the problem than seeking its solution.

In the first counseling session the minister helps counselees formulate a vision for the future—what the future will be like when the complaint is solved. From the first moments of counseling, they should define and work toward the goal, determining how they will get there.

The specific, concrete description of a problem and the aware-ness of its exceptions readily lead to the establishment of limited target goals, which are clear descriptions of the desired change or solution. The goals are chosen mutually by pastor and counselee. Both participate in identifying realistic and reachable goals which can be achieved in a short period of time. Critical to a successful outcome is that counselees not try to cover too much ground by trying to change too much, too quickly. Later, when these limited goals are reached, a new set of goals can always be established.

Two methods have helped me steer people from focusing on problems to forming a vision of their future. The first says to the person, "Tell me how you want your life to be different one (or three or six) month from now. Be realistic, recognizing work, family, and financial constraints. Also be very specific." Examples of possible responses include:

■ I will register for an accounting class so that I can get a better job in the comptroller's office.

■ I will join Al-Anon and learn how to live with my alcoholic husband.

■ I will join choir and men's club at church to help me get out and interact more with people, instead of staying home and feeling sorry for myself.

Another approach has been influenced by de Shazer (1988, 5). The *magic question* asks the counselee: "Suppose that you awakened tomorrow morning and your problem was magically gone, how would you know? If by magic the problem were no longer there, what would be different in your life? How would your family or friends know? How would they say that you had changed? How would I recognize the change?" After two or three sessions additional questions can be asked, such as: "Are there days when a little bit of the magic has occurred?" "How are these days different from before?" The purpose of secondary questioning is to help counselees realize that change is not only possible but is already happening.

Either approach helps individuals to conceive a new future and develop specific goals. Both can be discussed in the session or can be given as a written homework assignment.

The way counselees are addressed and the types of questions they are asked can contribute to helping them envision a new future and develop workable counseling goals. Most individuals in counseling tend to speak of their problems in the present tense. A subtle way to reframe their difficulties (see chap. 4) is to refer to them in the past tense. In addition, it is best to refer to counseling goals using "when" instead of "if." For example, say "What do you think *will* occur *when* you start to come home earlier from work" instead of "What do you think *would* happen *if* you start to come home earlier from work."

Married couples tend to describe their spouses in terms of their behavioral flaws. Such descriptions need to be altered. For example, the claim "He is not considerate" is better stated as "He does not pay attention to you when you want to discuss something." The counseling goal thus changes from altering a personality characteristic to making specific behavioral changes.

Some individuals in counseling only want to talk about problems; at each session they dodge any initiative to discuss solutions to their problems. With such persons, questions such as, "What is the difference between the times when the problem is better and the times when it is worse?" or the use of the magic question are apropos. Or ask "What will be the very first sign that change is on the way?" Most counselees tend to focus on the ultimate answer, when everything will be completely as they wish, and do not want to notice the first subtle signs of transition and growth. Such questions help to sensitize them to these nuances of change.

Some individuals think of the problem only as residing in someone or something outside of them. Inevitably the minister will make various suggestions to which they will answer "Yes, but . . ." Sometimes it is beneficial to compliment such counselees for their suffering, telling them you recognize that they still must have some sense of hope or they would not be there in front of you. It also is worthwhile to compliment them for being good historians of the causes of their problems (Berg 1991). The objective is to change their view of themselves and their thinking about the problem so they begin to see that they have some part in the solution.

Berg (1991) suggests the use of *scaling* or *coping* questions with especially challenging counselees. A scaling question might be: "If ten means that you will do *anything whatsoever* to solve the problem of fighting with your wife, and one means that you will just sit there and do nothing, where are you on a scale of one to ten? How about your wife, where would she say you are? Your neighbor? Your best friend? What will it take for you to go from five to six on the scale? What will it take for your wife to say that you have gone from five to six?"

In situations that to counselees seem completely hopeless, coping questions may be useful. "How do you cope?" "How do you get through the day?" "How come things are not worse?" "From what you have told me about your background, how are you coping as well as you are?" Such questions focus not on the problem, but on strengths that reside within the person that allow them to cope.

When counselees begin to describe their problems, other problems often come tumbling out. This snowballing effect is easily misinterpreted as a sign that long-term therapy or referral is necessary. The pastor does best not to allow the counseling process to become sidetracked onto problems other than those addressed by the target goals, however important they may seem. The minister simply suggests, "That sounds like something important. After we have achieved your goal, we can take up that issue if you would like."

Wells (1982, 12) puts it this way: "Implicit in the short-term helping process is the belief that change is most likely to ensue from a concentrated focus on a single but significant problem in living (and, conversely, the belief that much natural problem solving is weakened by attempting to deal with too many difficulties simultaneously)." Therefore, the pastor needs to help the counselee facing an assortment of problems to choose one or two goals as the highest priority. Because short-term counseling is limited by time, its goals also must be limited. Narrowing the focus to one or two small goals increases the likelihood that change will actually occur.

A final thought on goal setting: I have encountered many counselees whose previous experience in counseling was disappointing. In many cases, they came in for one problem but were treated for another which the therapist thought was more important. For example, an overweight man who wanted help in controlling his weight spent most of his therapy sessions reconstructing his relationship with his parents, especially his mother. The therapist thought that his family relationships were keys to his losing weight, but the man dropped out after more than twenty sessions because little attention was given to his overeating. Any pastorally determined goal needs to be related directly to the counselee's goal. Negotiate and mutually adopt a goal; if an agreement cannot be reached, then do not accept the person for counseling.

Develop a Plan

Frequently all that is needed to get counselees on the path toward resolution—no matter how complex or intractable the problem appears—is one small change, one small alteration in the way they do things. A corollary applies in this case: the larger or more all-encompassing the goal, the greater the likelihood that it will *not* be achieved. A vital task of brief pastoral counseling, therefore, is to develop a plan that can help counselees make small changes right away.

Developing a plan is primarily the responsibility of the pastor, even though it is constructed in concert with counselees. Goals are translated into specific tasks that parishioners can understand and perform. Two things are important to the success of this plan: first, individuals must comprehend the specific steps needed to address their difficulties; and second, the steps they take need to be achievable in a short period of time. Counselees need to recognize and believe that the tasks facing them are doable.

Remain Active in the Counseling

A proactive stance is required of ministers as they help parishioners with their problems of living. Although the skills of nondirective counseling are useful in establishing a relationship, the pastor should not be merely reactive, that is, the pastor should not just listen to the parishioner's issues. In brief pastoral counseling the minister cannot become sidetracked into unhurriedly developing rapport, listening passively, or taking extensive history—all of which can be a part of long-term counseling and which counselees often see as irrelevant to helping them solve their problems.

Together, helper and counselee select goals that will be the focus of counseling, but it is the helper's job to choose various interventions that will be used to achieve these goals (chaps. 4–11 will describe and illustrate several of these interventions). A proactive stance means that the minister selects the specific change procedures to be used.

Wells (1982, 9) defines the proactive stance well: "The change methods employed are structured, in the sense of comprising a series of steps (or phases) that break the process of change into component parts and guide the activities of both helper and counselee." Such methods are described well in the literature of pastoral counseling and psychotherapy. No minister or counselor could ever learn all the existing interventions, but every helper needs to have five or ten different counseling interventions at hand in order to address a variety of problem situations.

Assign Doable Homework Tasks

O. Hobart Mowrer once said, "It is easier to act your way into a new way of feeling than to feel your way into a new way of acting" (in Clinebell 1977, 171). One of the quickest ways to initiate change is to address and act on the specific issues in real life through the use of outside-of-sessions tasks, or homework. Ministers and counselees need to agree on these tasks, although the suggestion of appropriate homework assignments will usually depend upon the pastor's expertise. Ideas for homework frequently will arise as a natural part of the conversation, and the minister will translate the ideas into actual tasks that counselees can perform out in the real world (homework tasks are detailed in chap. 2).

Build upon Counselee's Strengths

People who are going through difficult times tend to ignore their own strengths and resources. Budman and Gurman (1988, 14) point out that the short-term-oriented counselor has "a health rather than an illness orientation. The brief therapist wishes to help the [person] build on his or her existing strengths, skills, and capacities." Brief pastoral counseling does not break down people's defenses, but builds up or energizes their coping resources and strengths. One of the quickest ways to help individuals feel better about themselves, thus enhancing self-esteem, is to get them to use some of their forgotten strengths. Neither breaking down defense mechanisms nor gaining insight into one's own defenses is generally needed to manage a problem. Helping persons through building upon their own strengths not only requires less time, but it is also *more humane* than breaking down their defenses. The focus in brief pastoral counseling is therefore less on pathology, problems, and explanations and more on competence, strengths, and solutions. It is to make specific changes in counselees' environment or in their particular ways of handling a problem. Changes in emotions or insights are secondary. As Franz Alexander has stated, "No insight, no emotional discharge, no recollection can be as reassuring as accomplishment in the actual life situation in which the individual failed" (Wells 1982). Both emotional release and insight are natural results of a short-term pastoral counseling process that builds upon individuals' own latent strengths.

In short, the *why* of human problems is not the focus: the *what* is. Discerning the specific behavioral changes that will be beneficial, and their achievement, is the real aim (Watzlawick, Weakland, and Fisch 1974). Building upon existing skills is the best—perhaps only—way to reach this goal. When people make specific changes in and for themselves, they experience relief from the painful stress and demoralization that accompany their problems.

A principal way to build upon people's strengths is to show them hospitality. The counseling session needs to be a place where counselees are welcomed, encouraged, and complimented for what they are doing well, not where their past wrongs or present pathology is dredged up. Near the end of the initial (and possibly sole) session, and before homework tasks are discussed, it is good to give counselees appropriate compliments. de Shazer writes: "The purpose of the compliments is to build a 'yes set' that helps to get the clients into a frame of mind to accept something new—the therapeutic tasks or directive" (1985, 91). Examples of appropriate compliments include the following:

- I'm impressed with how hard you have been working to improve your problem. Even though you have not achieved what you wanted, it is obvious you have given considerable effort to it.

- I would like to compliment the two of you on the extensive and detailed information you have given me regarding your son's behavior.

- It must have been difficult for you to come to my office today. I want to compliment you on your courage to be here and talk about these things.

TERMINATION

One advantage of short-term methods is that ministers terminate counseling more often than counselees. Brief pastoral counseling methods by definition apply to situations with less than ten visits, typically one to three sessions; thus from the opening of the first session, pastor and counselees plan for the end of their counseling relationship. The message needs to be clear: although continuing afterward as their minister, you only will spend a limited number of counseling sessions with them. O'Hanlon and Weiner-Davis (1989, 178) point out that

> one of the reasons therapists fail to terminate is because, even when there is no longer a problem, clients offer details of their lives which seem to merit intervention—a fight with a spouse, a bad day at work, a ravenous departure from a strict diet, and so on. However, we all know that ups and downs are a natural part of life. Therapy is not meant to be a panacea for all of life's challenges.

The purpose of the counseling is not to resolve all of people's problems but to make an initial breakthrough which will help them acquire some basic skills that they will need for continued development and growth after the counseling has ended. Even though pastoral care will continue to be offered, the special relationship found in counseling concludes.

In the case of Roger Pendley, the conclusion of the counseling relationship occurred gracefully. After her initial visit, Pastor Lin met twice with Roger and his family. In those two sessions, each family member expressed a desire to include Roger in family life and to help him make his difficult transition from living independently to joining their already functioning family group. Together they came up with a dozen ways Roger could contribute to their life together. For example, Roger, who for years had had a passion for gardening, could tend the neglected flower and vegetable garden that Gloria had started several years ago in a burst of back-to-the-earth enthusiasm. More importantly, Roger had been excluded from family meetings because the rest of the family thought he would not be interested; now he was to be included in the regularly scheduled discussions and would be given a voice in decisions that affected them all.

Pastor Lin met with Roger alone once more and found him a different person—more relaxed and at home. He even appeared to be hearing and seeing better. After this follow-up meeting, it was time to end the counseling sessions and return to their former pastor-parishioner relationship.

When the counseling relationship is being concluded, reviewing with parishioners the gains they made during counseling is important. These gains may seem obvious to helpers, but counselees may not see them at all or attribute them only to luck or to the minister's care and concern.

Reviewing changes achieved and skills learned also covers what issues were *not* addressed. Suggestions and strategies for the future are developed at this time. Frequently, discussing with counselees what they will do in the event that their problems reemerge is also beneficial. For example, in cases of persons who were suicidal when they first came in for counseling but are no longer, the minister would do well to predict that the counselee *will* feel suicidal again. This may shock the counselee, or they may not want to talk about it, but developing a plan of action for handling suicide ideas when they recur will give them a plan to follow (e.g., contact the pastor immediately, visit friends rather than stay home alone, return to the physician for more antidepressant medication). One of two outcomes usually occur from such discussions: if counselees never feel suicidal again, they will forget that those feelings were predicted; or, should they have such recurring thoughts, they remember that it was forecast as a normal and expected occurrence and begin to follow the plan that was developed. (Frequently the suggestion is made that they write their future strategy on a card to carry in their purse or wallet.)

Some individuals become anxious as the time for termination of counseling nears. They usually are feeling and doing better and fear falling back to old ways after counseling has ceased. They may bring up new problems or relapse into old ones in an effort to stretch out the counseling time. When these signals appear, at least two courses of action are available: First, review the gains they have made in counseling and indicate that although growth is a bumpy road, they will be able to travel it. Second, do not terminate the sessions immediately. If their fear of going it alone is pronounced, then the gentler way is to stretch out the time between visits and shorten the length of visits, finally setting up a meeting two or three months away to review progress. A good procedure is to schedule a follow-up meeting two to four months after the termination of *all* counseling in order to fine tune and reinforce changes that have been made. The pastor should be especially attentive to counselees when they see them in weekly church activities.

Finally, the minister needs to let people know that they can return for counseling whenever new or recurring issues emerge. Even though the present problems are in the process of resolution and the formal counseling relationship is ending, no one can know what new difficulties may emerge in the future.. One of the reasons brief pastoral counseling methods are so well suited to congregational ministry is that people can be sincerely assured that the relationship is not ending, only shifting, and that as a need arises, help will be available.

2

Working between Sessions

Naaman, commander of the king of Aram's army, had brought great success to his king. But Naaman was afflicted with leprosy and had tried in vain to find a remedy. When one of his servants reported that a prophet in Samaria could aid him, Naaman went to his king and received permission to seek a cure. He brought along a considerable fortune, about 750 pounds of silver and 150 pounds of gold, as a gift.

When Naaman arrived at the prophet Elisha's door, Elisha did not receive him. Instead he relayed a message to Naaman: "Go wash in the Jordan seven times, and your flesh shall be restored and you shall be clean."

Naaman was furious at this unexpected treatment. "I thought that for me he would surely come out, and stand and call on the name of the Lord his God, and would wave his hand over the spot, and cure the leprosy." Naaman wanted Elisha to wave the proverbial magic wand over him to effect an immediate cure.

Naaman's servants reminded him that he had already invested a great deal to make the trip and had spent much in gifts. He relented, washing seven times in the River Jordan as Elisha had instructed, and "his flesh was restored like the flesh of a young boy, and he was clean" (2 Kings 5:10-15, adapted).

Naaman did his homework—he came to the prophet for help, his helper assigned him a task, and he accomplished it. One of the best ways to predict how well counseling will succeed is to observe how well counselees do homework tasks between the first and second sessions. Individuals who take responsibility for changing their lives almost always take their out-of-session tasks seriously and complete them as they have committed themselves to do. Not surprisingly, they also experience positive growth and resolution of their difficulties. In contrast, those who do not do the tasks, or make feeble attempts at them, have little chance for beneficial change.

The real work of counseling does not happen in the one hour of the counseling session—where a safe, friendly environment is established—but in the other 167 hours of the week. Outside tasks, or homework tasks, are a way of extending the impact of the pastoral intervention and helping individuals do something about their problem. (With some individuals, I do not use the word "homework" when describing tasks they are to do between sessions because of the bad taste this word has left in their mouths from their school days.) The purpose of homework is to validate and strengthen the changes that have occurred within counseling and broaden the extent and impact of these changes in people's daily lives. Homework is a stimulus to action, carrying the benefits of counseling into the daily world.

Although the assignment of outside tasks is common in other modes of counseling, brief pastoral counseling has developed and refined the practice. Homework tasks include a variety of activities that counselees may perform between sessions. A side benefit is that such tasks help to shorten the pastoral counseling process.

HOMEWORK TASKS

The way in which the minister establishes homework tasks is critical to their accomplishment. The following are suggestions concerning the use of homework tasks.

Select Directly Related Tasks

It is vital to use tasks that are directly relevant to the goal of counseling. Although this may seem obvious, there is a temptation to work at "underlying causes" of problems and therefore to choose homework that focuses on the supposed underlying cause. This should be avoided in short-term pastoral counseling. Tasks that directly address the counseling goal usually make more sense to counselees than those designed to attack underlying causes and therefore are more readily accepted.

Develop Appropriate Level Tasks

Besides being directly related to the counseling goal, homework tasks should be neither too difficult nor too simple; otherwise, counselees will not derive the sense of accomplishment that is a major motivation for homework in the first place. Tasks should be difficult

35

enough to give a sense of mastery but not so difficult that they cannot be achieved. If the pastor is unsure about a person's abilities, easier tasks should be assigned. Also, individuals in crisis, the depressed, and those whose minds are muddled by a swirl of emotions will have more trouble accomplishing tasks; their homework should be less difficult.

Assign a Series of Graded Tasks

Sometimes tasks of increasing difficulty are needed. Appropriate homework for the male college student who is afraid of women students, for example, should probably not be to "go talk to several women this week." This may be too large an order for him. One appropriate first step for him may be to attend a club meeting on campus that includes both men and women (e.g., a campus Christian fellowship group). He would not have to say anything to anyone, but only attend and be a part of the meeting. Upon successful completion of this task, he might take more difficult steps in subsequent weeks until he is able to initiate a conversation with female students. (The number of steps this takes would depend upon the extent of the student's anxiety.)

Plan Mutually Developed Tasks

Ordinarily, homework options need to be negotiated rather than simply prescribed. With the exception of some crisis situations (Stone 1993) or paradoxical interventions in which tasks need to be assigned prescriptively (see chap. 4), it is preferable to discuss possible homework tasks with counselees.

When talking over specific homework options, using presuppositional wording is helpful. For example: "*After* you go to the choir practice at church, you will have to tell me how well your conversations with other choir members went and exactly what you had to say." Not: "*If* you go to choir practice." "If" denotes a condition of uncertainty. Counselees in such instances are more likely to accomplish tasks if they have taken part in choosing them.

Convey the Importance of Homework Tasks

The more importance individuals attach to doing specific homework tasks, the more likely they will do them. Frequently little more is required than explaining the value and relevance of the task. Sometimes counselees are helped in accepting a task assignment if it is presented as an *experiment* rather than as a task to be undertaken for the rest of their lives. However homework tasks are assigned, they need to be structured so that they make sense to the counselees.

Recognize Accomplished Tasks

Some individuals have difficulty believing they can ever do anything of value. As a result, they discount any tasks they accomplish as "dumb luck" or the result of someone else's effort (e.g., the pastor's support). A sense of mastery and the resulting feelings and actions thus do not occur, and one of the major values of the homework is lost. Therefore, ministers need to help counselees recognize the counselees' part in accomplishing the task. This cannot be overemphasized because some people fight off recognizing their own personal achievements.

Practice Homework Tasks

Some counselees do not do their homework because, despite all appearances, they lack the requisite confidence or skills. For example, in marriage counseling couples commonly are told to express feelings to each other, to get them out in the open. This is good advice, but what if the person does not know what a feeling is, let alone how to express it? The homework will not get done—or, if attempted, will fail—not because of resistance by the counselee, but because of poor structuring by the helper. The pastor in such a situation needs to help people become conscious of what a feeling is by expanding their emotional awareness. Such persons can then be taught the skills of communicating feelings, practicing them in the counseling session. Modeling the behaviors in the session and using behavior rehearsal (see chap. 7) will increase the likelihood that the task will be performed outside the office.

Specify Task Details

Resistance, confusion on the part of the counselee, or lack of specific details prevent the accomplishment of a homework task. The details for implementing a task outside the session—"go wash in the Jordan seven times"—need to be worked out in detail. For example, if a couple needs to communicate more effectively about how they spend their money, the minister needs to help them decide how long their talk session will be, what days and at what time of each of these days their talks will occur, how they will handle disagreements, and so forth. If they fight about who should start talking, then a resolution needs to be negotiated. They also will need to look realistically at ways in which the talk sessions could fall apart and develop ways to handle situations such as conflict or when one spouse "forgets" the session or when a child gets sick.

All of this sounds complex and involves more detail than many pastoral counselors might personally prefer. After a number of years of practicing brief pastoral counseling that incorporates homework, however, I still marvel at how inventive counselees can be in sabotaging tasks. One thus needs to be specific and detailed when setting up homework and realistic about obstacles to its accomplishment.

In family counseling, make sure that every family member who comes for counseling gets a task to do, even if their job is to stay out of the task. "The task should be structured like any other piece of work. Someone is needed to supervise, someone to plan, someone to check to see that it gets done, and so on" (Haley 1976, 58).

A final suggestion: Have note cards (three-by-five-inch are ideal) available on which counselees can write the details of their homework and take with them. Because they write out the tasks and keep the information with them, they will be less likely to forget or become confused about the tasks. Writing down the tasks helps to prevent misunderstandings that may occur and cements counselees' commitment to the homework.

Commit to the Task

After the task has been discussed in detail and its benefits considered, ask counselees if the task makes sense. Pause for discussion and ask about their willingness to do the task. Such inquiries help determine the extent of their commitment.

If they appear at all hesitant, comment on their indecisiveness, and ask how the task could be changed so that they will feel more comfortable with it. After some conversation, renegotiation of the homework is usually possible. Resistance to the task does not bode well for its accomplishment—or for the achievement of the counseling goal. Commitment to the homework task is critical to its accomplishment and to the success of the counseling effort as a whole.

Heighten Learnings

Do not assume that because troubled individuals have successfully completed certain tasks, they automatically will gain the desired benefits; counselees do not necessarily have the hoped-for insight (Archimedes' "ah-ha!" experience) or the ability to learn from doing a task. Depressed individuals are a good example. Because most people who are melancholic cognitively distort reality in some manner (often seeing themselves as worthless or inadequate), when they do accomplish something beneficial, they usually do not recognize it. Burns and Beck (1978, 120) suggest that individuals who are depressed tend to sustain such negative beliefs despite substantial evidence to the contrary. Thus the minister is responsible for determining whether counselees are missing the lessons offered by the tasks and helping them reflect on their accomplishments. A step-by-step review of the task is frequently all that is required, with the minister prompting them to look at what they did while recognizing and affirming their courage, creativity, savvy, or initiative in doing so.

Plan for Uncompleted Tasks

Sometimes when giving homework to counselees, it is useful to ask them to think of ways in which they may attempt *not* to do the task. For example, what if they receive an unexpected visit by out-of-town friends? What if they need to work late all week? Such queries sometimes help to forestall problems in task performance.

It may be helpful to speak discouragingly about the task while presenting it as "I believe there is a way to deal with your problem, but I'm afraid you are not going to like it." This method works especially well with rebellious individuals, who may react against the discouraging words concerning the homework . . . and make sure they do it! With counselees who are antagonistic toward another individual, a helpful phrase can be added: "However, I believe your spouse (boss, parent, or whomever) will like this solution even less."

Despite preparation and forethought, however, expect some individuals not to complete their homework tasks. (Naaman did not depart for the River Jordan until those around him convinced him to go ahead.) Plan for uncompleted tasks and have a strategy for handling them. Be careful to avoid two extreme strategies. First, ignoring an uncompleted task is not beneficial. Opening each counseling session with a discussion of the homework suggests to counselees that their tasks should be taken seriously. Second, admonishing persons in an angry, parental manner for not completing their homework is equally unproductive. Rather, locate what caused the failure in an even and adult manner, ask what happened, and pause for discussion. Then, determine whether the problem is due to resistance, inability, confusion, or the like. You might say, "Okay, let's see what happened, so that you can accomplish the counseling goals that brought you here." Pause here for discussion, but do not press or indulge them. Afterward, you might say, "Does the task still seem like a sensible one, or should it be changed?" The next question will be: "What do you think can be done so that this task will be accomplished?"

Some people try to get the helper angry at them, which again would confirm that nobody cares about them, that there is no use in ever doing homework tasks because they are beyond help. A pastor who is easily drawn into this game needs to rehearse such situations with a friend because counselees are sensitive to the helper's attitude and can sense unexpressed or unacknowledged anger.

In the end, some counselees will do the homework tasks, others will change the tasks to better suit themselves, some will do the opposite of what was proposed, and some will avoid doing them. The strategies outlined above increase the chances for the first and second, more favorable outcomes.

TYPES OF HOMEWORK

The following is a sampling of types of homework tasks that can be used in brief pastoral counseling sessions. These suggestions are by no means exhaustive, but offer a taste of the inventiveness that is possible in creating homework tasks.

Use the list of tasks only as a starting point for creativity and experimentation. Develop new types of tasks and tailor them for each situation. Explore new ways of helping people move into action. When helpers err in brief pastoral counseling, most do so on the side of not intervening enough, not risking enough, not exploring a wide enough range of homework tasks or other methods that will help counselees grow and achieve their counseling goals (Driscoll 1984; Egan 1990). Three types of homework will be discussed: assessment tasks, action tasks, and paradoxical tasks.

Assessment Tasks

One way to communicate that the minister takes counseling seriously and expects counselees to participate actively is to assign homework at the first session. A useful form of homework at this early stage is one that assists helpers and those being helped to better understand the problem. Assessment tasks actively involve counselees in exploring their problems and the directions they need to take to bring about their resolution.

Assessing and recording a specific behavior. One assessment activity is recognizing and recording a specific behavior. Behavioral theorists point out that people frequently do not judge accurately the extent of a problem (e.g., how often a seven-year-old picks a fight with his five-year-old brother or how many times one spouse nags the other). The first job, therefore, is to establish a *baseline*. Both pastor and counselee need to know exactly the scope of the problem. Some people may ruminate about it from morning to night, exaggerating its extent or frequency. This information later allows pastors and counselees to know how much improvement has occurred. Charts, golf counters, diaries and logs, even pennies moved from the left pocket to the right are all ways of measuring the frequency of a behavior.

Keeping a journal. Another type of assessment homework is keeping a journal, especially one that focuses on a specific issue. The college student who had difficulty talking to women could use a journal to record all his reactions to interchanges with women, no matter how brief. He could then bring the journal to the counseling session and read extracts aloud, thus helping minister and counselee together to formulate the next steps to be taken.

A journal is also useful for noting changes that occur as a result of counseling; it is especially helpful for those counselees who are hypersensitive to their problems and who ignore or forget the changes they have made. Using a journal is also a classic discipline of spiritual direction, a way of marking the movement of the Spirit in one's life.

41

It helps individuals to heighten sensitivity to their relationship with God.

Reading books or articles. Reading books or articles also serves the assessment task. Such reading should not be passive but have a specific purpose. Counselees read a particular piece and underline each statement or dog-ear each page that describes themselves. In the succeeding session, minister and counselee review the underlined sections. The minister asks questions about the marked sections, such as how they refer to the counselee or what examples of them are in the person's life.

When counseling depressed individuals, I frequently have them read Paul Hauck's *Overcoming Depression* (1973). I urge them to assess their own depression and determine whether it arises from the "poor you" or "poor me" or "bad me" that Hauck describes (see chap. 10).

Videos can be used similarly by asking counselees as they watch to look for situations that are similar to their own. In fact, videotape bypasses a drawback common to reading assignments, which is that only active readers are likely to accomplish them. When I first began using readings, some people had not read their assigned book by the next session. I then realized that many people simply do not read—some do not even read one book in the course of a year. I then began referring magazine articles and videos to the counselees, which usually they will read or view.

Noting and recording exceptions. Another assessment task that corresponds to the overall orientation of brief pastoral counseling is noting and recording exceptions. It asks counselees to observe what already is working well in their lives and what they want counseling to build upon. Examples of possible assignments include: "List what you do in place of snacking at night that keeps you from overeating." "Record what you did when you *overcame* the urge to snack." "Notice what in your marriage that you want to continue."

Action Tasks

Doing something actively to assist in the resolution of a problem is the second group of homework tasks. The range of possible activities is limited only by imagination and creativity. The following are specific examples of the types of action tasks that can be useful.

New experiences. Homework tasks that provide new experiences are especially helpful for fearful and overly anxious individuals. Such tasks help them stretch in directions that they ordinarily would not choose. They may be as little as suggesting to a proper man that he wear a loud tie or jeans and a T-shirt. It could also mean urging someone to try a new food, such as tandoori or tofu. Anything that gets individuals to venture away from their habits by doing new and adventuresome things can be of benefit.

Interpersonal action tasks. Pastors also can implement interpersonal action tasks, such as talk sessions for couples in marriage counseling who desire to open channels of communication. Such sessions have to be structured carefully and in great detail, or the communication problems that brought the couple to seek help may dominate the sessions and nothing will be accomplished. Family councils can be established that allow all family members to air grievances, resolve difficulties, and develop more constructive relationships.

Many individuals come to counseling with unfinished business in past or present relationships; they need to face these relationships and say what needs to be said. Assertiveness training helps some people handle difficult relationship situations. Writing a letter to a parent (alive or deceased) or other significant persons from the past is another way interpersonal baggage can be lightened. (I usually have counselees bring drafts of such letters into the session and, after discussing them, decide if they really want to send them.)

Do something different. Encountering a married couple or family in which one person has a complaint against another (and claims to have "done everything" to effect change) is common. That person's way of responding to the other's behavior is usually stuck in a rut. In such cases, the person's homework might be: "Do something different."

For example, a wife's primary complaint against her husband is his drinking. "I've tried everything to get him to stop," she complains, "and nothing has worked." In fact, she has not tried everything. Her reactions when he comes home drunk follow a fairly typical pattern which she does not recognize.

To the person with the complaint, one might suggest: "Your task this week is to do something different. Each time Jim comes home inebriated I want you to do something you have never done before—no matter how bizarre or unusual it is. The important thing is that it be *different*." For instance, the wife may ignore her husband totally where in the past she would have either argued with him or helped him; she may change into her best clothes and leave the house without telling him where she is going; she may sit down and start playing the piano or go out and wash the car or wash windows while accompanying herself with energetic singing; the possibilities are endless.

The minister does not prescribe what the person is to do, only that it be a new, preferably surprising behavior. An advantage to this form of homework task is that it can be used with a wide variety of problems and the helper does not need to know the exact complaint. This homework task succeeds because it breaks the routine responses that characterize dysfunctional relationships; it breaks the vicious circle of action and reaction that two people are caught in (de Shazer 1985).

Self-improvement tasks. Another type of action homework is self-improvement tasks. An example of this kind of task is taking up running or an organized exercise program. Learning relaxation exercises (see chap. 11) or enrolling in a parenting class are other examples. Numerous disciplines in spiritual direction can be adopted (Stone 1988). Joining appropriate self-help groups (e.g., Alcoholics Anonymous or Al-Anon) are some of the most useful forms of tasks that counselees can adopt. With people who are doing especially well in dealing with their problems, prescribing a scheduled relapse (e.g., returning to watching TV instead of spending time with people) is sometimes useful because they will ultimately have setbacks anyway and such an assignment helps them be prepared. In all action tasks, counselees do something that directly addresses their problems and gives a sense of mastery because something concrete is being accomplished.

Paradoxical Tasks

Paradoxical tasks respond to the resistance to change found in counselees. People sometimes resist the things they want most. Instead of fighting against the problems, the minister joins counselees in making slight alterations to the symptoms of the problem in ways that cause them to lose their potency. Haley (1976, 52) categorizes homework tasks according to two different ways of presenting them to counselees. They are: "(1) telling people what to do when the therapist wants them to do it, and (2) telling people what to do when the therapist does *not* want them to do it—because the therapist wants them to change by rebelling." Haley's second group, which therapists sometimes call paradoxical tasks, is the focus of this type of homework.

In a sense, paradoxes are one part of every problem. For example, trying to be something that conflicts with one's present state is paradoxical. A specific example is asking a tense person to relax. Impossible! The more a person tries to relax, the more tense he or she becomes. The same is true for the insomniac. The more he or she tries to go to sleep, the more noticeable the cracks on the ceiling and the sounds in the building become. A paradoxical task is telling an insomniac to stay awake. The minister, in effect, is prescribing the counselee's own symptoms (Watzlawick et al. 1974). When insomniacs try to stay awake, they no longer consciously will themselves to sleep, and as a result they can often sleep.

The best homework is frequently to suggest to counselees that they do something they already do—only to change the structure of it slightly. This is called *symptom prescription* (see chap. 4). The couple that fights most of the time is told to fight—but only at certain times. As Haley (1976, 71) points out, "People do not like to fight or make themselves miserable because someone tells them to do so." Paradoxical tasks often capitalize on this natural rebelliousness of individuals.

A woman who had been married fourteen times did not want to tell her present husband about all of her previous marriages. When psychotherapist Milton Erickson asked her, "Don't you think you ought to tell him about the other marriages that you haven't mentioned?" she responded in the negative. Then Erickson said, "Well, that's your answer and *stick to it.*" The woman did not like taking orders from men, so she told her husband. Erickson believes that "as long as they are going to resist, you ought to encourage them to resist" (Haley 1973, 234).

Individuals who become paralyzed when applying for jobs can be told to apply for jobs that they do not want and then can deliberately blow the interview. A woman to whom I suggested this tactic applied for a job as a delivery driver for an auto parts store. In spite of what she did to make a poor impression, she was offered the job.

45

It intrigued her so much that she accepted it temporarily until she could get the job she wanted. She ended up enjoying it so much that she stayed with it.

A man who is afraid of being turned down for a date may be assigned to get turned down on purpose two times before the next session. Such tasks can stir up strong feelings, but they are developed to "challenge the dire need for conventionality" and "help clients evaluate the accuracy of their predictions of how the world will react to them" (Walen et al. 1980, 226).

Paradoxical tasks are a powerful and effective form of home-work but assigning them requires considerable expertise. Chapter 4 deals specifically with paradoxical strategies and will discuss a number of paradoxical tasks ministers can use.

Homework tasks are vital in pastoral counseling, especially for short-term counseling. They spread the influence of the counseling session to the rest of life; they actively engage counselees in the management of their own problems by helping them learn new skills and more effective ways of functioning; and they distinguish those who really want change, like Naaman, from those who only pretend to want change.

3

Focusing on Outcomes

The final goal of all helping is *action* that brings about problem management—making a decision, accepting a loss, learning a new skill, finding a job, maturing in the faith, deepening a relationship, or some other beneficial outcome. Thought-out and decisive action leads to growth. In brief pastoral counseling, the need for action emerges almost immediately.

Because the time that counselees are usually willing to devote to a counseling process is limited, action needs to be directed toward specific, identifiable predicaments in their daily lives. In one form or another, problem management methods are used in most types of counseling, whether brief or long-term. In brief pastoral counseling, problem solving is at the center of the care offered. Therefore, problem management is the focus of this chapter. Problem management can be used by ministers in their counseling and taught to counselees as a means of dealing with their present and future problems.

Joe and Linda Hernandez cared for each other, but for the past four or five years had had increasing difficulty communicating with one another. They recognized this difficulty and were open to suggestions for addressing it. They had even attended a marriage enrichment seminar sponsored by their church. Held at a rustic retreat center complete with fireplace and nestled in the pines by a rocky stream, it was an uplifting experience. They learned specific communication skills which helped them to speak clearly and to understand each other, thus relieving what had been a key problem in their marriage.

After they came down from the mountain, however, Linda and Joe made an unsettling discovery: Having become better communicators and having clearly told each other what they wanted to see changed in their relationship, they were no closer to resolving their differences. The problems were still there—all they could do now was communicate better about them.

Knowing about a problem but being unable to manage it is a common difficulty addressed in brief pastoral counseling, especially among relatively sensitive, insightful people. Education in problem management methods usually helps such people. Joe and Linda were fortunate that their parish priest was both knowledgeable and experienced in problem management methods and was able to teach them enough about problem solving so they could begin to help themselves find compromises and solutions for their differences. By teaching problem management skills in counseling, a basically sound marriage was spared from being bogged down in frustration. Like relaxation and communication skills, problem management skills benefit individuals and couples in their daily lives.

Success in particular occupations requires developing skills in problem management. Attorneys and businesspeople, for example, are frequently effective problem managers because they are able to resolve problems rapidly and sensibly. Many people—including some counselors and ministers—do not have as systematic a set of skills in this area. For them particularly I will outline the following five-step model of problem management which I call the GRACE method of problem management, and which I have found effective in my practice of pastoral care and brief counseling. GRACE is an acronym for the five tasks of problem management:

Goals
Resources
Alternatives
Commitment to action
Evaluation

Even without trying to place too much weight on the acronym, the aptness of its message is surprising: facing and coping with our problems is done with confidence in God's presence, love, and help before, during, and after the problem has been rectified. "My grace is sufficient for you, for my power is made perfect in weakness" (2 Cor. 12:9).

GOALS

Changing the focus of the helping from negative problems to positive solutions and goals is the first step in problem management. The magic question (see chap. 2) or questions that cause counselees to claim a new vision of the future (see chap. 1) can help to make this transition. They cause counselees to avert their eyes from difficulties and look at specific ways in which their lives can be different. Looking for exceptions to their problems can help counselees find a direction as well—not an entirely new direction, but determining what is already working for them and committing to do more of it.

Goals have at least seven key elements (Berg 1991). They are:

■ Goals must be considered important to counselees.

■ Goals should describe in concrete, specific, and behavioral terms the change that is desired. They need to be developed so that success can be measured.

■ Goals are best kept very small—not "going to college and graduating," but "making a list and ranking five possible college courses."

■ Goals need to be described as the infancy of a new vision for change. In brief pastoral counseling, the minister's intent is to start counselees on the right track and then get out of the way. After change is initiated, the other ministries of the church— worship, fellowship, spiritual guidance, service—are ready to continue supporting and encouraging former counselees on their way.

■ Goals must be realistic and doable within a short frame of time.

■ Goals should describe the *presence* of something other than the problem—not the absence of something. Thus, for the couple who say they fight all the time and want to stop fighting, the goal may be that they go to the movies, share work at home, and so forth. The goal should not be stated simply as "Stop fighting."

■ Goals involve considerable effort for counselees even though they may not seem difficult to helpers. Therefore, counselees must be told to prepare to work hard at achieving them.

For example: Suppose the problem with a family is that a void was left when the couple's last daughter married a military pilot, and the daughter and her husband moved to another country. The couple's goal is to fill a void now that their home is empty and only long distance parenting is required. A specific goal may be to begin gathering information about starting up the mail order business that the couple had talked about for years, but never seemed to have time to start. As simple as this goal sounds, it uses all seven key elements and has a good chance to succeed in beginning to give the couple the meaning they seek.

RESOURCES

The next step is taking inventory of the internal and external resources available in working toward goals. Internal resources include inner strengths and skills, coping methods, and successful past experiences with problem solving. Everyone has gone through problem situations in life, negotiating many of them successfully. When a person reports little or no success, ministers can then share their own experiences. Such sharing can prompt others to recall their own experiences.

External resources are found in people's environments: church; community groups and agencies; family and friends; schools; money and assets; and so forth. These resources offer much in the way of advice, assistance, moral support, and gratification as people handle difficult situations. An inventory should include how a person's resources might be used and what difficulties might result if they are called upon.

ALTERNATIVES

After establishing goals and assessing resources, the counselee and minister can brainstorm the possibilities available for reaching a solution. Together they list all of the alternatives—the wacky as well as the wonderful. The pastoral carer may need to begin or assist in developing the list in order to illustrate to the individual (whose thinking may be clouded) how many courses of action are possible. Better, however, is when most of the ideas come from the person with the problem.

The brainstorm list then needs to be narrowed. Obviously inappropriate alternatives are weeded out. Because several courses of action may achieve the same goal, it is necessary to consider other aims that the person is trying to accomplish through change. The individual's ethics and values must also be considered as possible actions are sifted.

Considering the person's ethics and values is more important than many helpers recognize. For example, one counselee who was in the midst of a divorce and wanted to get custody of his four-year-old son was advised by his attorney to kidnap the child because "possession is nine-tenths of the law." This advice, however, ran contrary to the father's values regarding the treatment of his child and he rejected the attorney's advice. A person's work schedule, family obligations, and finances also may influence or express a person's values.

After the initial elimination process, the effectiveness of the remaining courses of action is weighed. The minister can now provide information from her or his own experience and background that might assist individuals in evaluating how well each alternative will assist in reaching their desired goals. In some cases a combination of two or more alternatives may be just right for resolving a situation; therefore no single idea should be dismissed too quickly. Listing and selecting alternatives is a collaborative effort in which pastor and counselee together choose those that are most likely to be fruitful. The counselee, of course, will take as much initiative and responsibility as possible.

COMMITTING TO ACTION

When the list of alternatives is narrowed to a few (or even one) that appear to have a high chance of success, counselees need to make a firm commitment to embark upon the chosen course. The action may (and often should) be broken down into small, concrete, and easily attainable steps.

Taking action is essential in problem management, but, at this point, people often resist moving forward. They may forget to do what they decided upon, become too busy, or may be afraid of the consequences of change. The minister needs to encourage individuals in any way possible to begin acting because only then can they experience positive change and start feeling better (see chap. 2). If resistance persists at this point, then referral to a psychotherapist is in order.

EVALUATION

An ongoing part of the problem management process, done more consciously once concrete initiatives are under way, is evaluation, or review and refinement. Judging the effectiveness of changes made toward achieving stated goals is an ongoing task. When the evaluation reveals progress, the counselee will be encouraged to continue. When the review discloses lack of progress, the goals or alternatives may need fresh scrutiny or change.

Goals, resources, alternatives, commitment to action, and evaluation: the five-step GRACE method itself is subject to refinement. The best way to teach problem management methods is to help counselees resolve the problems they bring, and then to review what they have done and what they have achieved. Although problem management can be taught in the office or classroom, people learn it best from concrete experience while being guided through problems of their own. In brief pastoral counseling, counselees not only work at managing their problems but they also learn a way of addressing future ones through use of a model like the GRACE problem management method.

Part Two

PROBLEMS
&
INTERVENTIONS

4

Marital Distress

∽

Paradoxical Strategies

Sylvia Gardner was filled with guilt, which was reason enough for another visit to her pastor. She intoned a litany of recent sins, most of them seemingly minor infractions. She had not sent a thank you note to her neighbor who gave a birthday luncheon in her honor. She did not visit her uncle when he was in the hospital. She cut in front of another woman in the supermarket line. She borrowed a book from a friend and lost it. She spoke rudely to the clerk in the post office. She forgot her sister-in-law's birthday. She felt resentment toward her boss. She called in sick when she was really just overly tired. Her pastor had become so wearied by Sylvia that her "sins" were pooh-poohed, and she was instructed not to worry.

Sylvia was thirty-seven years old, married to her husband Dean for fifteen years, and the mother of twin twelve-year-old boys. When the Reverend Carol Geddes arrived as her church's new pastor, Sylvia felt desolate; she was certain she could never tell her deepest secrets to a female minister. But Sylvia was so troubled by guilt that she increasingly withdrew emotionally from her husband and sons. Dean finally urged her to make an appointment with Pastor Geddes, who suggested that Dean accompany Sylvia.

The Gardners had barely settled into the pastor's comfortable chairs when Sylvia began her usual recital of sins—now backlogged for some time. Unlike the previous ministers, though, Pastor Geddes did not minimize Sylvia's sins. She took them at face value and accepted the premise of guilt. Not only that—she assumed there was more to what Sylvia was telling. "You seem so filled with guilt," she said. "Are there other guilts that are also troubling you, sins that are hard for you to talk about?"

Neither Sylvia nor Dean had expected such a reply. Sylvia was used to defending her guilt in front of Dean and others who argued her innocence. This pastor was asking for more.

Sylvia paused, then came up with a few earlier improprieties that she had already shared with the previous pastor, but really more of the same. Pastor Geddes waited. After a full minute of silence that seemed like ten, there followed a tale of two girls, Sylvia and her best friend, Allie, each thirteen years old, who had explored their sexuality together. Their experiments involved some mutual masturbation—which Sylvia labeled "unnatural" and "unforgivable."

Sylvia had never told her husband about these childhood sexual adventures. Dean now sat impassive and did not seem too terribly concerned. Her one previous confidant had tried to tell Sylvia that such sexual experiences were a normal part of adolescence, and that even if they were sins, surely God would forgive her. Sylvia, unconvinced, thought God could never absolve her guilt.

Pastor Geddes realized that even gently debunking Sylvia's beliefs about sexuality or emphasizing the forgiveness of God too quickly, without taking seriously her sense of guilt, would lead nowhere. Such strategies likely had not worked before and certainly would not work now. Pastor Geddes needed a different approach.

She chose to use paradoxical strategies of reframing and symptom prescription to respond to the problems presented by the couple. Paradoxical strategies encompass a variety of interventions that have been developed somewhat independently by clinicians from several schools of psychotherapy in recent decades, especially among those practicing family therapy.

Reframing, the more cognitively oriented of the two types of paradoxical strategies, involves accepting counselees' problems (and their beliefs about them) at face value—not trying to argue about them as others most likely have done (Bandler and Grinder 1979; Seltzer 1986; Watzlawick, Weakland, and Fisch 1974). The counselee's *frame*, or how the person sees reality, is accepted to the point of the troublesome feelings, thoughts, or behavior. After that, the helper begins to question the troublesome aspects of the person's reality, but always from within the counselee's frame.

Pastor Geddes therefore did not respond with some sort of resurrection theology that would instantly announce Sylvia's forgiveness and minimize her sense of guilt. She accepted that Sylvia had sinned in many ways—beyond even the sins she first presented—which led to the revelation of the deeper and, to Sylvia's mind, "unpardonable" sin. Here, in discussing the unforgivable nature of adolescent sexual experiences, Pastor Geddes began to question Sylvia's beliefs, or frame: "You have stated how important your faith as a Christian is to you, Sylvia," Pastor Geddes said, "and how important forgiveness is for each person, and how much you want and need God's forgiveness. But tell me, why do you think Christ died on the cross for everyone but you? What made you so special that you are above his forgiveness?" As they talked of God and forgiveness, Sylvia began to question her own frame. Although she wanted to talk of some sins as unforgivable, when Sylvia spoke of her understanding of God, she acknowledged that God's grace encompasses all that humans do—even her "unpardonable" acts.

The other type of paradoxical strategy Pastor Geddes used with Sylvia and Dean was *symptom prescription*. A symptom is the problem behavior or experience that the counselee wants to eradicate. Whereas reframing focuses upon changing how people think about events, symptom prescription seeks to bring about a change in their behavior. Counselees are asked, or directed through prescription, to maintain their symptoms. In time, the symptoms disappear as a result of trying to hold onto them.

Even though Dean was concerned enough about his relationship with Sylvia to accompany her to the counseling session, his contributions amounted to nods, smiles, a pat on Sylvia's shoulder, and a few monosyllabic responses. Pastor Geddes decided to enlist him into active duty by involving both of them in a prescription.

Sylvia and Dean, Pastor Geddes instructed, were to choose a particular one-hour period each day, perhaps after dinner while the boys were doing their homework, when Sylvia would tell Dean all her sins in great detail. She was to give it full play, holding nothing back. His task was not to placate or ignore her, as he had come to do in recent years, but listen carefully, attend to everything she might say, and even heighten her confessions by asking for more details. Furthermore, he was to suggest additional ways in which she might be guilty—as many as he could imagine. "Between sessions," Pastor Geddes directed Dean, "try to notice everything that Sylvia might be guilty of which you can bring up at your next day's meeting. Be very thorough!"

After just a few evenings, Sylvia found this prescription an onerous task, began to rebel against Dean's suggestions of further guilt, and even started somewhat indignantly to defend her innocence.

WHY PARADOXICAL STRATEGIES?

Why is it that the straightforward help we offer does not always work? Why does our well-meaning help, no matter how elegant, sometimes fail to be effective? A variety of explanations might apply, but when ministers offer counsel to individuals, couples, and families, the counselees sometimes seem to do everything possible to negate the offered help. It is as if they are holding on to their symptoms for dear life even while voicing a willingness to do whatever is needed to bring change.

One reason counselees do not follow straightforward counseling interventions is due to basic human nature. Sin can be seen in many shapes and forms, and one of its forms in counseling is a pessimistic negativism, a rebelliousness which manifests itself in resistance to change, however keenly desired. Paradoxical counseling strategies respond to this nature of humans to resist the things they want most. Instead of trying to oppose certain problems, the helper goes along with them. Instead of trying to fight problems, the minister joins the symptoms, making slight adjustments to them so that they lose their potency.

It is not bad that Sylvia feels guilty, but she was putting a large load of guilt into tiny vessels of petty sins. She needed to connect her guilt with its source. "Virtually all paradoxical strategies are designed to counteract stubbornly maladaptive responses by not actively contesting their existence. . . . By ironically joining forces with nonchange, they may effect a fundamental shift in counselee attitude that clears the path for productive—and self-initiated—change" (Seltzer 1986, xii).

Paradoxical strategies are used in pastoral counseling and most schools of psychotherapy (Capps 1990; Seltzer 1986). Seltzer discovered forty-seven terms used to describe paradoxical strategies. The two basic distinctions of paradoxical strategies I prefer are reframing and prescription.

Frames and Reframing

Goffman (1974, 10) describes frames as definitions of situations that are "built up in accordance with principles of organization which govern events—at least social ones—and our subjective involvement in them." Stated more simply, *frames* are the way we perceive events or circumstances and are the guidelines that shape reality for each of us. Frames may be seen as patterns by which we put together and interpret information and experiences. They are like templates placed over our experiences so as to give them meaning. Even in similar situations, when these templates or frames are changed, then feelings, thoughts, behaviors, and attitudes are also changed.

Reframing offers a different interpretation of experience. The helper suggests other ways of perceiving the same event. Watzlawick and associates (1974, 95) explain that to reframe "means to change the conceptual and/or emotional setting or viewpoint in relation to which a situation is experienced and to place it in another frame which fits the 'facts' of the same concrete situation equally well or even better, and thereby changes its entire meaning."

The meaning of an event depends upon the frame of the person experiencing it. If the helper can raise any doubt about a person's frame ("Why do you think Christ died on the cross for everyone but you? What made you so special?"), then the old meaning of the event erodes and another meaning appears (Bandler and Grinder 1979, 1). A person who entertains the slightest doubt about even one aspect of his or her frame, who considers another way of looking at the event, will have difficulty returning to the former point of view. Reframing helps counselees look for exceptions to the premises that are the foundation of their frame. When holes in a frame are discovered, hope is engendered because counselees can begin to visualize a future without the problem.

Unlike cognitive restructuring, which may try to argue counselees out of illogical or irrational points of view, reframing has the helper adopting the counselees' perceptions. After all, people believe their existing frames. Ministers should initially concur with the frame (in Sylvia's case, guilt over many small transgressions), up to the point of the problem (the unpardonable sin or the seeming inability to receive forgiveness). After that, they can help counselees question their frame not from the outside, but from within it. They then find a fissure (a crack in the logic, perhaps) in the frame's undergirding. The task then is to get counselees to reflect on this opening. The space widens, new light is cast on the situation, and the possibility for healing is engendered.

Reframing interventions characteristically startle, confuse, or unnerve when they are first put to counselees. For example, imagine the likely reaction to labeling a couple's bickering as "your way of showing affection." Papp (1980, 46) describes such interventions as producing a "perceptual crisis" which makes it harder for a family to "regulate itself through a symptom" and helps it move toward a new means of self-regulation.

Reframing is more compelling, and the possibility for rapid change more likely, if family and close friends cooperate. They also need to adopt the frame of the counselee (e.g., Sylvia's guilt over many small sins) and not try arguing them out of their frame. To be of help they also need to agree with the new frame (e.g., that Christ's redemption was for everyone and for all sins).

Prescription

Part of pastoral care's legacy from the first part of the twentieth century is prescription, but of a somewhat different sort than is described in the case of the woman with excessive guilt. These early prescriptions were based on Scripture or tradition. Often counselees were directed to read passages of Scripture and take them to heart. Sometimes prescriptions were given without a thorough knowledge of the situation or sensitivity to individual needs.

Subsequently, nondirective pastoral counseling helped ministers become more sensitive to people's situations, but lost the art of pre-scription (Stone 1988, 23-25). Indeed, many clergy have been taught to avoid making decisions for counselees, even in the assignment of homework tasks. With such a background, some pastors may be uncomfortable in using prescription in brief pastoral counseling. Their discomfort may be eased by the knowledge that directing counselees to do certain things, much as a physician prescribes med-icine or a teacher assigns homework, can be an effective way of helping people change.

One of the most useful types of prescription is to *prescribe the symptom itself* or some element of it. This enables the minister and counselee to gain control over the symptom so it can be changed eventually. Symptoms are not happenstance; they are artfully de-veloped in order to realize some purpose in the family system. No matter how crazy it seems at the moment, at some time in the past the symptom worked for the person and probably for the family. Within a family some form of collusion maintains the symptom which is exhibited by the "identified patient." Seltzer (1986, 98) puts it this way:

> What might practically be identified as the family's symptom may be regarded as the key instrument of its resistance. One primary function

of symptom maintenance in therapy is its enabling the family to assert control over the therapist. The family can conveniently strip the therapist of his or her potential power to foster change by adhering precisely to those interactions that have kept the maladaptive behavior in place.

Family nurtures the symptom. Resistance to change is great and can be insidious. Because many people in counseling seem impelled to counter most of the helper's suggestions, one of the most useful approaches is to prescribe their symptomatic behavior.

Symptom prescription can take many forms. In some cases counselees should practice the problem symptom exactly as it exists. Other times the minister can ask the counselee to exaggerate the symptoms or make some minor change in how the symptom is practiced. In all cases the helper gains control over the problem symptom that was perceived to be out of the counselee's control. Practicing the problem behavior is the route toward changing it. Many people do not like to be told what to do—not even things they already do! To quote Milton Erickson: "The idea is to make a laborious task out of whatever the habit [symptom] is—you turn a vicious habit into an awful inconvenience which the [counselee] is willing to give up" (Rossi, Ryan, and Sharp 1983, 264).

The helper's imagination can offer creative prescriptions. One of my pastoral counseling supervisors suggested I use a symptom prescription that was rather exotic but worked surprisingly well with a particular couple—and has worked on several occasions since. (Caution: this is neither for the faint of heart nor for couples in abusive relations.) A husband and wife had come for counseling because of their frequent, heated fights that erupted into yelling and screaming. Their prescription was very simple: whenever an argument escalated into a battle, they were to take off all their clothes, make swords from folded newspapers, and continue their fight in the nude. The couple was not told to stop fighting; instead they were told to alter slightly the way they fought. Then and since, no couple to whom I have assigned this task has been able to continue fighting after removing their clothes. Most end up laughing. It might be said that I have not helped them solve the problems precipitating their fights, but they have been given a little breathing space, a chance to see their situation differently (seeing it from a different frame)—and that is a major step toward resolution. There are countless other prescriptions, most of them less bizarre, which ministers can use to help people reframe their situations (see Symptom Modification below).

PARADOXICAL INTERVENTIONS

Paradoxical strategies can be implemented in many ways in addition to those already presented. Some emphasize changing how people think and are based on reframing; others direct people to enact a part of their symptom and are based on symptom prescription; and others emphasize both to such an extent that they cannot be categorized as one or the other. Typically it is best to utilize both reframing and prescription when using paradoxical strategies with counselees. The following is a sampling of procedures especially suitable for ministry which will give the reader a taste for the possibilities of paradoxical strategies.

Symptom Modification

Milton Erickson (Haley 1973, 197) treated an adolescent girl who still sucked her thumb. Erickson did not prescribe the predictable deterrents—they had already failed. Instead, he instructed the girl to suck her thumb for twenty minutes each evening in front of her father and after that for twenty minutes in front of her mother. She was to do it in as aggressive and noisy manner as possible. The parents were told to ignore her completely, and were not to become upset by the thumb sucking or comment on it. Rather than try to get her to stop the thumb sucking as so many had done before him, Erickson modified the way she went about it. She was supposed to suck her thumb, but only in the way instructed: in front of each parent and for a specific time period. When a symptom is changed into a duty, most children tire of it quickly. No longer "forbidden pleasure," or a weapon to use against parents, it loses its appeal, as thumb-sucking did for Erickson's young counselee.

Symptom modification is a form of symptom prescription wherein the problematic behavior is to be done in a slightly altered way. For example, the time or place where it is performed may be changed. Seltzer (1986, 118) states that "the resultant disruption, however minor, of the symptom pattern may have a cumulative effect similar to removing a single pillar from a building's foundation." It starts a change and puts counselees in greater touch with their abilities to change or control their problem.

In addition, if counselees can be inspired to change their symptom in any respect at the bidding of the helper, they are more likely to ascribe to the helper the power to change it in other ways as well.

By following the instructions of the minister to modify the symptom, counselees establish a pattern of assenting to what the helper suggests. This compliance, or "yes-set," sets the stage for further requests by the minister to do additional tasks to bring about the desired change.

Several years ago, Phil, an early retiree in his late fifties, was seen by his pastor for help. Because of a medical condition, Phil had lost the ability to control his flatulence. A polite and proper man, he avoided any situation in which someone might become aware of his ailment. Over time he dropped out of most of the clubs and social activities he had enjoyed. Old friends did not understand the reason for his withdrawal and thought he had become antisocial.

Various brief pastoral counseling methods, including symptom modification, were used to address Phil's fear of flatulence in public. Phil hated the idea of symptom prescription when it was first presented to him ("How can that do any good?" he asked), but with some persuasion he agreed to try it. His task was to go to several meetings and events at church and *wish* that he would pass gas, which he would naturally do anyway. In fact, he was to try to increase his flatulence. The motto attributed to Benjamin Franklin was endorsed: "Fart proudly."

Symptom modification had the effect of neutralizing Phil's fear. He had been petrified of "breaking wind" in public, but had little need to worry about it when his goal was to try to do it. In Phil's case, symptom modification diminished his fear enough to allow him to go out in public again. It did not stop his flatulence, of course; it only changed his frame—and his degree of apprehension.

Symptom modification is obviously not a method for every brief pastoral counseling situation. It works best with people who are not too rigid to laugh at themselves, and the minister has to believe in its efficacy. This is no time for tentativeness; suggesting any form of symptom prescription takes some *hutzpah* if the counselee is to have confidence that it will work.

Confusion

Milton Erickson found that when he made a statement that counselees found hard to understand or confusing, he was able to deflect their resistance when they sought definition or clarity. When pairing confusingly erudite statements with clear ones, he found counselees more eager to agree to the clearer statement—perhaps out of relief or embarrassment for not understanding the other. In this method, a crucial counseling intervention is prefaced with deliberately confusing words. It assails counselees' rational minds with ambiguous statements, often making them more positively inclined toward the helper's clearer suggestions. This method bears some resemblance to hypnosis in that it bypasses the conscious beliefs that box people in and allows them to consider ideas that they otherwise might dismiss out of hand.

The confusion technique can be used, for example, in gaining a person's agreement to bring her or his spouse to marriage counseling. Spouses offer endless excuses as to why their partner will not or cannot appear for counseling. When the need for the other spouses' participation in marriage counseling is first brought up, and before resistance is mounted, confusing or obtuse statements about human nature can be followed with the suggestion that the partner attend. For example, the pastor might say the following:

> Our religious faith is founded upon principles that tie suffering with hope, which causes the strength we see in the Christ and in the earth to come together in a union which is sought by all, much like the marriage union when strife and grace come to us. (Slight pause.) Therefore, I believe it is important that your wife come and be a part of the counseling and I will plan on her being here the next time we get together.

Startled by the contrast in clarity between the two statements, many counselees will find it easier to consider asking the spouse to attend. The desire to cease being bewildered by the new frame (the confusing statement) causes the person to latch onto the next intelligible particle of information (ask your wife to come to the next session).

This often happens in real life. A friend told me recently of having to travel by train from Cambridge, England, to a remote Scottish island by way of London and Glasgow. The trip had at least six legs. He had been on the train from London all night when he arrived in Glasgow at 6:30 A.M., needing to find his way to another train station and get some breakfast in the process. He located a restaurant that was open, and when he ordered from the menu, the waitress replied at length in an accent he could not fathom. He asked her to repeat herself. Still no comprehension. Finally he picked out the words "number three" and "quicker." With great relief he switched his order to breakfast number three, not even knowing what it was, but grateful just to get something to eat.

The confusion method also is useful when counselees need to do more of the work in counseling or accomplish their own problem solving. Years ago, a pastoral counselor used this method with me quite successfully, and I did not catch on until years later. He would tell me, "You were saying . . .," and then stammer or hem and haw until I would impatiently help him out and finish his statement. I am convinced that at times he purposely misstated or confused what I was talking about so that I would correct him and go into greater depth about what I was saying, which was his goal. He was using the confusion technique skillfully.

Ministers are trained as counselors to make increasingly clearer statements to individuals as the counseling progresses, so the confusion technique can be hard to embrace at first. But consider using it. In the right cases it can be a persuasive brief pastoral counseling tool. I know this from personal experience not only as the counselor, but also as the counselee.

Convince Me That You Should Change

Ministers frequently encounter a particular type of person who is mildly depressed, passive, and perhaps overweight, who can list a thousand ways in which she or he has tried to change, none of which has worked. Cynthia was such a person. Her children had graduated from high school and left home for college and careers. She was depressed at a low level, forty pounds overweight, and said she needed to make some changes, such as going back to school or getting a career outside her home. But she was resistant. She could state all of the reasons that prevented these changes from occurring.

Many times Cynthia had told others what she had told me— that she needed to do something useful in her life since her children were now away and that she should lose weight for her health. Friends and family were supportive of her desire to bring about these improvements.

Cynthia expressed in counseling that she wanted to do something about her weight first so that she would look more presentable when looking for a job. I knew she had tried many diets and that she could explain why none had worked. I caught her off guard by asking: "Why should you lose weight?" I explained that about 95 percent of people who lose weight gain it back and so most likely it would fail. I told her that I hated the thought of her failing one more time, and that perhaps she should reconsider even trying to lose weight.

Cynthia was stunned. She did not know what to make of her minister saying she should reconsider losing weight. When she caught her breath, she said, "Well, I suppose you are right, but . . ." and then tried to convince me why she really ought to lose weight and how going to Overeaters Anonymous would give her the group support she needed. I listened skeptically, trying to point out reasons that might keep her ideas from working. She tried even harder to show me how they would. Finally, I said, "I don't think I can agree with your suggestion to lose weight until you have had at least a week to consider it."

Needless to say, she came back the next week announcing that she was going to deal with her overeating and that she had attended her first Overeaters Anonymous meeting the night before. Her frame was turned upside down. Before, she had become adept at finding reasons why she could not change. Now she was trying to convince me that she was capable of making the same changes. She lost weight, returned to school to update her teaching certificate, and now is teaching. Cynthia may sometimes wonder why I was not more supportive of her goals, but she achieved what she wanted and was satisfied.

This technique challenges counselees to convince the pastor about their motivations for changing, rather than vice versa. It disarms them. Agree with their defenses, concur that change is not possible (even though they say aloud that they want it), and change the game plan. The element of surprise is on the pastor's side. This method works best in situations where change is slow in coming. When change occurs, do not praise or act too pleased about it. Rather, continue to be slightly baffled by the counselee's shift in behavior. Neither take nor accept any credit for the change; after all, they changed in spite of such "skepticism."

This paradoxical intervention can be used in at least two other ways (Capps 1990, 37). First, suggest to counselees that change is a very slow process and that for the moment they should do no more than think about it. This can energize people who are defending themselves against change. Second, treat as inconceivable any notion that the counselee *could* change by quizzing: "How in the world do you think you could do that?" Either assume that they are not able to make the change or wonder aloud why they would ever want to consider making the change. This paradoxical strategy is a good intervention for brief pastoral counseling because it motivates people to change. It allows people to make changes rapidly and to bypass resistance to change.

Dereflection

Ministers and counselors are bedeviled by counselees who have devoted little or no time to consider their situation and in whose lives reflection is almost absent. In contrast, others reflect too much. They ponder their situation endlessly and are obsessed by it.

Dereflection is a technique that requires such people to reduce their consideration of their situation which would give them time for more favorable thoughts. Counselees are instructed that whenever they find themselves ruminating about their problems, they are to think instead of positive activities that can benefit their lives, and then choose to do one. They are to purposely change their thoughts and do something more constructive. (Even the proverbial cold shower, when literally taken, is a dereflection method that counters sexually obsessive thoughts.) Dereflection is not the same as telling a friend to accent the positive. Different dereflective thoughts and activities are explored and experiments conducted until productive ones are discovered.

Sometimes dereflections can be given as a prescription by the counselor; other times counselees use trial and error to find the thoughts and activities that will replace their ruminations. Dereflection helps them to break the bonds of their obsessive reflections and to give their thoughts, time, and energy to more productive solutions. (See chap. 8 for other interventions useful for people with obsessive thoughts.)

Benevolent Sabotage

An important lesson for people with teenaged children to learn is that parents have little control over what adolescents do. Parents may reason, coax, cajole, beg, and issue ultimatums, but the teenager can choose to defy them. Benevolent sabotage (Watzlawick, Weakland, and Fisch 1974) is a paradoxical strategy designed for such situations. In it parents state what they expect of their children, but follow with the frank acknowledgment that there is nothing they can do if the teenager does not comply: "Timothy, I do not want you to invite your girlfriend over to the house after school when we are not here, but if you choose to do so, then there is nothing we can do about it."

Benevolent sabotage is appropriate when sanctions no longer work and parents are frustrated. It requires that parents use the technique cheerfully and with a straight face, without sarcasm or rancor, just stating the obvious: "We know we cannot compel you to do this."

Watzlawick and associates suggest that the benevolent sabotage technique can be extended beyond admissions of powerlessness to active steps. Parents can lock the doors to the house at the time their adolescents are due home, then go off to bed. When the children arrive, the parents open the door, sleepily apologizing for having locked them out. No speeches or recriminations. Whether parents will accept these more active measures will depend upon the extent to which the minister feels comfortable suggesting them and on the parents' own sensibilities.

Benevolent sabotage is useful for adolescents who will not clean their rooms, come home on time, attend classes at school, or study or those who spend time with the wrong type of crowd, or who generally do not obey their parents. Their frame is changed because there is nothing against which to rebel or fight; they cannot struggle with someone who has already admitted defeat. The helpless cannot be resisted. As a result, adolescents often become more willing to cooperate. The frame is also changed for the parents; they do not have to be frustrated about their rules being disobeyed because they realistically recognize that they cannot be enforced.

Relabeling

People label themselves or others and then live their lives according to the labels. Labels determine how people feel about themselves and the degree to which change is possible. A person tagged as "lazy," for example, does not have as good a chance for change as one portrayed as "having many gifts that need only to be harnessed." These labels come from different frames: the former provides little chance for growth whereas the latter provides some hope.

Relationships can stagnate in the paralysis of negative labeling. Sometimes the most important thing the minister can do to help a marriage is to assist the couple in relabeling key characteristics of their partnership. Relabeling induces a change in the frame of reference against which an event is judged; thus the meaning or the value given to it is changed without any actual alteration in circumstances.

For example, if the husband who perceives his wife as "so anxious about her career that she is never able to loosen up and enjoy things" can shift to "she focuses on her clients as her way of showing concern for the family," then tensions can be eased. Likewise, if the wife who sees her husband as "a workaholic who never spends time with us" can relabel his long hours as "dedication to his work and a concern that his family have a comfortable and secure life," then she has a better foundation for a turnabout in their relationship.

When using relabeling, suggest an alternative name for certain characteristics in a person or relationship: depression becomes sadness, anger is changed to hurt, and any symptom of one family member is interpreted as something positive he or she is doing for the family. The new label describes the characteristic as accurately as the old label (or more so) and casts it in a more positive light. Not a sugar coating—the old label had an overly negative tint to it and the new label has a more realistic, positive one. Relabeling reframes the situation and communicates the possibility of change.

The paradoxical strategies described above can help troubled individuals perceive situations differently and act in new ways. Most helpers will find one or two methods among these methods that they can adapt to their own brief counseling ministry. Some helpers may be uncomfortable using these techniques; they are certainly a deviation from traditional, nondirective pastoral counseling practices. Others may consider paradoxical counseling methods more advanced than the methods described elsewhere in this book. Nevertheless, paradoxical strategies help many people achieve their own goals faster than many other methods and more rapidly than nondirective approaches. Capps (1990, 50) argues that these strategies

> are designed to out-maneuver the dysfunctions which are causing pain and discomfort, allowing the creative energies of the counselee to emerge instead. The techniques work precisely because the therapist respects the counselees and regards each one as a unique and special

individual. Jesus out-maneuvered the demons precisely because he had deep respect for the persons who were in their control.

These brief pastoral counseling interventions are designed to be for counselees, helping them to achieve the personal goals that initially brought them into counseling. As such, paradoxical strategies are a good addition to other methods of brief pastoral counseling.

5

Parenting Issues
∾
Reinforcement Methods

It's hard being a parent. Raising children seems never to go as planned—and certainly not as outlined in many parenting books. Precious bundles grow into loud, climbing, mischievous toddlers who bite their siblings and decorate the walls. Book-packing school children graduate from action figures, Barbie dolls, and Tonka trucks to rock music and an awareness of the other gender. And then the teenage years guarantee to try the patience of many a law-abiding parent.

Frequently, the minister is the one called upon to referee what parents cannot manage. Over half of the brief pastoral counseling situations to which pastors respond are marriage or family issues, and most of the problems are not the easy ones. A family usually will not seek counseling until the situation seems desperate. Many times I find myself wondering what prompts families to tolerate all that pain for so long before coming for help. Did they not know how much easier it would be if they had come sooner? On a bad day I feel like throwing up my hands, telling them to seek help elsewhere or solve their own problems or just grow up. Frustrating and difficult as it can be, ministry to families is part of a minister's calling.

A TOTAL APPROACH

Overarching in importance when dealing with parent-child difficulties is to help parents recognize and value the infinite worth of their children. Without such an appreciation of worth, the children too frequently become little more than problems, hindrances to their parents' realization of their own aspirations.

Although the focus of this chapter is reinforcement principles— methods for strengthening and maintaining desired behavior or weakening and stopping unwanted ones—two other counseling practices prove helpful for addressing problems with children: communication training and systems theory. These approaches provide a good backdrop for the use of reinforcement methods. Together they furnish a total approach to helping children and their parents.

A newspaper article reported a recent study claiming that parents spend on average fifteen minutes talking with their children each day, fourteen minutes of which is giving orders! Programs that teach parents how to *communicate* more effectively with their children have been especially beneficial for parents who have little time to talk to their children. The work of people like Thomas Gordon (1970) in parent effectiveness training is particularly useful for teaching parents to listen to and value what their children say. Gordon and others have helped parents to show empathy to their children and listen to them, rather than just tell them what they are supposed to do. Many communication programs have been developed by churches and counselors; these programs usually are taught in classes for parents and can form the basis for good preventive pastoral care. These same methods also can be taught in counseling sessions and serve as a foundation for the use of reinforcement methods at home.

A *system* in counseling theory is a group of individuals that functions as a whole. *Systems-oriented marriage and family counseling* emphasizes the interrelatedness of the various activities and events within a family; what Father does and says to Mother affects not only the marital relationship but also the child-parent relationship. Neither people nor problems exist in isolation; they are part of larger systems. The spiritual, mental, emotional, physical, and interpersonal functioning of each member of a family is intricately tied to all other members. What happens to one member sends shock waves throughout the system (Clinebell 1984; Haley 1976).

Systems theory presumes that problems are the family's way of adapting to what is happening in the environment at any particular time. A problem that causes a member of the family to seek help is seen as a symptom of the family's adaptation to life events. Because families tend to repeat themselves, the way a particular family adapts to a situation may be similar to the way previous generations of that family responded to similar situations.

For example, when parents come to counseling with a troubled child, the pastor frequently discovers that the marriage relationship has pressing problems in addition to those with the child. When the marriage as such and the family as a whole begin to function more acceptably, many of the symptoms identified with the child seem miraculously to be resolved.

Reinforcement principles have sometimes been inaccurately viewed as mechanistic or negatively manipulative, but when used together with communication training and systems theory and with a keen sensitivity to children's rights and values, they can provide an effective total approach for brief pastoral counseling of children.

PRINCIPLES OF BEHAVIORAL CHANGE

Reinforcement principles form a way of helping parents assist their children change troublesome behaviors. Sometimes the way parents discipline is to yell, scream, berate, or threaten. Other times a problem is ignored until it cannot be overlooked any longer. Still other times, parents can catch their child being "bad," while being unaware of how often the child is acting in an appropriate way.

What follows are the principles of reinforcement theory and some specific ways of implementing them to help change children's bothersome problems. Like the communication methods mentioned above, these principles can be taught in parenting classes or can be individually tailored to the family in counseling. Classes are especially beneficial in brief pastoral counseling because successful reinforcement methods generally require more than the two or three sessions common in parish counseling—closer, in fact, to ten sessions, which is the upper limit of brief pastoral counseling. Arranging for parents to learn these principles in a church or community education class reduces the amount of time needed for counseling.

Reinforcement principles sometimes need to be taught as part of a family's counseling sessions rather than in separate classes. In these instances, the parents (after assessment) learn what principles apply to their situation, how to carry them out, and what changes to discuss with the child. Specific examples of how the principles can be used with children will be given below. These principles also apply to adults. In brief pastoral counseling, the principles can be used with a wide variety of people and situations. Many principle apply to the strengthening and maintaining of desired behavior in children. The first four concepts discussed below are especially effective in this regard.

The Positive Reinforcement Principle

The *positive reinforcement principle* bespeaks age-old wisdom: a child's specific behavior will improve or will increase in frequency if every occurrence of that behavior is immediately rewarded. If, for example, a child wipes his or her wet feet before coming into the house, and the child is thanked and told how much this is appreciated, then the child has been given positive reinforcement. Giving the child a snack after cleaning her or his shoes is another example of positive reinforcement.

Counselors distinguish between primary, or *extrinsic*, reinforcers (the snack) and secondary, or *intrinsic*, reinforcers (the thank-you that encourages the child's sense of pride). Primary rewards might be food, beverages, snacks, and toys—all of which are especially effective with younger children.

Secondary reinforcers such as praise, hugs, gold stars, medals, and trophies have also been found to be quite effective with children. Saying things like "That was a well-organized talk"; "You did a good job taking out the trash"; and "I like the shirt you picked out" are examples of secondary rewards. These and statements like them foster in children the desire to make an extra effort the next time or to repeat the behavior.

Parents should be urged, whenever possible, to *catch children being good*, rather than catching them being bad (scolding and punishing). Most parents ignore their children when they do what they approve, but immediately react when their children act problematically. The best way to increase the frequency of appropriate conduct is to recognize it instead of ignoring it. This can be done by using a primary or secondary reinforcer. If parents learn nothing but this one basic principle in brief pastoral counseling—to catch their children being good rather than bad—then this would be a giant step forward in their child rearing.

The Negative Reinforcement Principle

Negative reinforcement makes sense intuitively: a child's behavior will improve or increase in frequency when the occurrence of the desired behavior is rewarded by the cessation of a negative consequence. For example, a usually careless son receives negative reinforcement for hanging up his jacket and putting his boots away if he is excused from drying dishes that evening. This negative principle functions much like the positive one, except that instead of receiving a prize, the child is spared something disagreeable. The negative reinforcement serves a positive function in stabilizing desirable actions.

The Premack Principle

A behavior desired by the parents but not by the child can be strengthened and increased by making access to one of the child's favorite activities dependent upon performance of the sought-for behavior. Parents who may never have heard of "premack" are doubtless familiar with the principle, which is sometimes called "grandmother's law." Examples of this "law" are: "You don't get a piece of cake until you eat your vegetables"; "You can go outside and play as soon as you have finished cleaning your room"; "You can sleep at Mary's house tonight if you get your homework done first."

The premack principle can also be a self-imposed incentive. Often during the summer months I write while at a cabin in northern Minnesota, where the walleye bite well in the evening. For me, evening fishing is contingent upon my completing a certain amount of writing each day. When my writing pace slackens, the thought of hooking into a four- or five-pound walleye encourages me to press on. I do not apply the principle rigidly, but it is a form of self-discipline that works well for adults as well as children.

Intermittent Reinforcement

When behavior is well established by regular reinforcement, encouragement to maintain performance can continue, but with decreased frequency. Intermittent reinforcement means that the desired behavior continues to be rewarded, but on a reduced basis.

When a child learns a new activity (like hanging up clothes), continuous reinforcement is best: every time the activity is performed, it is rewarded. Once the activity is well established, however, switching to an intermittent schedule of reinforcement is beneficial and can improve the child's performance.

Conduct that is continually reinforced may stop quickly if the reinforcement suddenly ceases. If the schedule of reinforcement is stretched out gradually, however, so that increasing performance is required for the same reinforcement, and if the child cannot predict when reinforcement will occur, then the behavior is likely to become habitual.

Seven-year-old Jenny was pleased with the compliments and special favors she received each time she cleaned her room. Her parents also were happy with her performance, but after a discussion about intermittent reinforcement, they decided it was time they stopped the continuous rewards. They did this by spacing out the reinforcement schedule, at first giving her continued words of praise but fewer special favors. After a while, when Jenny no longer expected special favors for cleaning her room, they praised her less frequently. Note that positive reinforcement was still given for the cleaning she did, but came less frequently and at unexpected times. For the child, intermittent reinforcement works something like a slot machine: the jackpot could spew forth with the next coin played. The child also develops a sense of satisfaction from the accomplishments he or she makes.

The Punishment Principle

Just as the principles mentioned above can be used effectively for strengthening and maintaining a desired behavior, other principles will effectively weaken or stop unwanted ones. The first of these is *punishment:* a child's action can be weakened if it is followed immediately by a negative consequence or the removal of a positive consequence.

Most parents need little incentive to pursue the punishment principle. Parents have spanked, berated, nagged, yelled at, scolded, hit, and ridiculed their kids. In short, punishment has perhaps been the primary if not only way in which many adults have sought to mold the character of the younger generation.

Sometimes this type of punishment works, but other times it can backfire. The advantage of spanking six-year-old Mark and telling him not to punch his brother is that for the moment, Mark stops punching his brother. The disadvantage, aside from the apparent hypocrisy of inflicting pain as punishment for inflicting pain, is that the result is not permanent. Once the memory of the punishment fades even slightly, the highly reinforcing satisfaction Mark gets from hurting his sibling takes over again. *Smack!*

Punishment can be effective when a child has learned a desired way of acting and is able to do it well, but has not stopped the inappropriate behavior. Punishment, however, often encourages the development of escape or avoidance actions that are sometimes worse than the original problem, such as developing bad-me feelings. The punished child frequently finds a different, sneakier, and more passively aggressive activity with which to resist the parent.

Should parents refrain from punishing altogether? Not necessarily. For centuries punishment was the primary mode of control in child rearing. Recently, in the Freud-Spock era of so-called permissive child rearing, children often were allowed to do what they wanted and had little parental interference. With no new method of control to substitute for punishment, the permissive approach proved unsatisfactory. Some children floundered without guidance or discipline from their parents, acting in ways that were not only upsetting to their families and society but were also harmful to themselves. The methods described in this chapter offer a more constructive alternative.

Some forms of punishment, if used sparingly and thoughtfully, can be beneficial in child rearing. One of the most helpful, often called the "time out" method, has been used in a wide variety of settings and is easily taught to parents. It is similar in some ways to the older "go to your room and stay there until you have a better attitude" method. Time out is different in that it is explained to a child beforehand and the punishment is applied only for previously detailed offenses. It usually involves taking the child out of his or her normal environment for a short period of time—perhaps five minutes—to a dull room in which neither amusement nor an opportunity to continue the troublesome behavior is available. The purpose of the time out method is to remove any possibility of reinforcing the undesirable activity. Such punishment, of course, should be part of a concurrent positive reinforcement program.

The Satiation Principle

If a child is allowed (or required) to perform a behavior until tiring of it, then the behavior will become weakened. This principle may be new to some parents.

Take, for example, Wayne, a nine-year-old boy who set fire to the vacant lot next door. For a moment he was the hero who discovered and reported the fire, but he did not expect to be caught so easily. When his mother called her minister, a rather novel punishment emerged. Producing three big boxes of wood farmer's matches and a three-pound coffee can, she told Wayne: "I want you to light every single match, blow it out, and put it in this can." Fantastic! he thought. But by the time he had emptied one box the fun was gone, and he yearned to be with his friends. Wayne told his mother that he had lit enough matches and would never start another fire, but she insisted that he light all of them, one-by-one. It took a long time. He became very tired of doing it. Since then, Wayne has not set things on fire.

Not all problem behaviors are stopped so simply, but the principle of satiation can be a useful method for weakening unwanted activities.

The Extinction Principle

To decrease the frequency of or stop a certain action, it is helpful to arrange the child's environment so that he or she will receive no reinforcement for it. This could require considerable mental effort because parents often have a knack for doing things backward. For example, when the three-year-old is playing quietly with the five-year-old, a parent might breathe a sigh of relief and scurry to get some work done or just collapse for a few minutes of rest. When the children begin to fight again, the parent yells at them. This means that parents ignore them when they are peaceful and shower them with attention when they are disruptive. The opposite approach is needed. It is much better to praise the children for their quiet play and, unless they are hurting each other seriously, to pay no attention to their scraps.

The Incompatible Behavior Principle

A child's misconduct can be weakened if incompatible conduct is rewarded. Parents have used this concept for generations. Using this concept, parents set up an either/or situation for the child in terms of time or substance.

Many people have tickled their children or clowned to make crying toddlers laugh. A counselor will advise parents that rather than scolding or spanking a child caught playing with an electrical outlet, they should simply divert the youngster's attention to something more interesting.

Three-year-old Randi loved to sing. She also loved to get in trouble just when her mother was in the middle of a demanding household task. The instructor in Randi's mother's parenting class suggested that at such times, the mother initiate a sing-along to engage Randi, which would be incompatible with Randi's unwanted behavior. After one week the mother reported that she was getting tired of repeatedly singing "Twinkle, Twinkle, Little Star," but that Randi had been peacefully preoccupied with the song and stayed out of trouble. (The advantage of singing as compared with, say, reading, was that the mother could carry on with her task at the same time.)

Parents do not need to be defeated by conduct that is inconsistent with their values or sense of well-being. They can seek to displace it by behavior that is incompatible from the standpoint of the child's own interests or time frame.

The Cuing Principle

Certain behavior principles are useful more for developing new behaviors than for encouraging or discouraging existing ones. Three such principles are particularly worth mentioning and will be discussed in this chapter.

A new way of acting is learned when a cue is received immediately prior to the occurrence of the hoped-for behavior. Parents have long cued, or prompted, their children in regard to manners.

When we were trying to teach our three-year-old daughter table manners, we prompted her to say "please" and "thank-you." Once she knew the words, we could ask, "What do you say?" and she would obediently say her pleases and thank-yous, but with little energy or meaning. Then one afternoon while out for a drive, we purchased three instead of our usual two ice cream cones—a whole cone for our daughter Christine. When she realized she would have a cone of her own instead of sharing one, she leaned forward in her car seat and exclaimed with enthusiasm, "Thank-you, Daddy!" She said it with such joy and meaning that it brought tears to my eyes. She had learned the meaning of thanks. (Of course, she continued to need occasional cuing—after all, we often say thanks as much out of consideration for others as from heartfelt gratitude.)

Cuing can be used for many behaviors, and can involve either verbal cues ("say thank-you") or physical cues (a hand on the shoulder in church to remind a child who is just learning to be quiet during the worship service). After a cue is given and the desired behavior follows, it is important that the parent reward the child with praise, a hug, or some other positive reinforcement.

The Shaping Principle

Rewarding successive approximations of a desired behavior will assist a child in learning new behaviors. Like adults, children need encouragement and a sense of success to keep trying.

Seven-year-old Richard was not as well coordinated as some children. His father Leo, a high school letterman, was determined to make his boy into an athlete. When they played baseball in the backyard, Leo would throw the ball faster than Richard could handle it. The boy would get frightened and want to quit playing. This angered Leo, who would call Richard a sissy and throw the ball even harder, until his son fell or was hit by the ball and went crying to his mother. Richard's mom would get angry at Leo. Everyone became upset, and Richard was learning not to play ball, but to fear it.

The situation was causing stress on the family, and they brought it up with their pastor, who suggested that Leo's demand that Richard "be a man" was too narrowly defined. Leo needed to be more willing to let Richard be himself; the child could not be a carbon copy of his father. Leo seemed willing to reconsider his attitudes.

In the meantime the pastor explained a way of teaching children to play ball (in itself a worthwhile goal) by successive approximation. Leo was first to roll the ball gently along the ground until Richard learned to field it well, and only then roll it toward him more firmly. Next, the father was to toss the ball underhanded, again gently, and reinforce his son every time Richard came even close to catching it (not just when he actually caught it). Leo was to gradually increase the speed and difficulty of the toss until Richard learned to catch. (Needless to say, this last stage would be omitted for a younger child who is not yet able, developmentally, to catch a ball in mid-air.)

The same process was to be repeated with batting. In this way the boy could learn at his own pace, without fear, rather than at the pace his father, a natural athlete, remembered having learned. Richard would also develop enough skill so that he could later make his own choices about whether to participate in athletics. He could decide from a position of competence and freedom, not from a position of failure and fear.

The Modeling Principle

Sometimes a child learns a new way of doing something when he or she observes a prestigious person performing it. The importance of models for learning has long been recognized in most areas of life.

Using this principle in Leo and Richard's case: to further help Leo in teaching his son to play ball, the pastor suggested that if Richard had a baseball hero it would motivate him further in his learning process. He also recommended that Leo invite Richard to attend a professional baseball game. If he chose to go and enjoyed it, then he might develop heros among the local stars in repeated outings. A child frequently emulates a hero: taking jumps off the front porch like a favorite motorcyclist or eating the breakfast of a decathlon champion.

As an adolescent, our daughter Christine was a great admirer of long distance swimmers, particularly women. When an English Channel swimmer was much in the news, Christine swam to an island far out in the lake—something she probably never would have accomplished at our urging.

Modeling is an important principle for parents. Like cuing and shaping, it can be especially helpful in learning new ways of acting.

THE COUNSELING PROCESS

Parents are usually receptive to reinforcement concepts and will be eager to work at them. Use of these methods with children will alter somewhat the pattern of traditional counseling procedures, especially long-term procedures.

Early forms of child counseling, usually long-term in nature, had the therapist seeing the child alone. Later it was realized that parents should be involved in the counseling process. This sometimes led to the formation of parent groups, and therapists would counsel the parents separately from their children.

Counseling for children later advanced tremendously with an approach to counseling that dealt with entire family units rather than isolated individuals. The approach quickly proved its usefulness as helpers discovered the importance of working with the whole family in the counseling process—a "systems approach" that ministers have known for generations. Observing the interaction of all family members is not only beneficial for helping the pastor assess the problem, but frequently the entire family's style of relating has to be altered if the child's actions are to be changed.

Although seeing the whole family initially for assessment, the pastor using reinforcement principles in brief pastoral counseling subsequently may choose to work primarily with the parents as the leaders of the family because they hold the key to any change in the children. The parents are taught systematically to apply the above-mentioned principles of reinforcement to the specific problem or problems they are encountering with their children. Because the child's environment is actively, if unwittingly, reinforcing certain actions at all times, neither the child nor the pastor is in the best position to bring about change. Parents are also the most important single factor in that environment. In effect, the minister using re-inforcement principles in short-term pastoral counseling serves as an educator, a consultant to parents (and teachers if necessary), assisting them in regaining control of the family environment and helping the child to resolve his or her problems.

The process of brief pastoral counseling as it relates to children's problems begins, as in the case of adults, with assessment. The specific behavior needs to be defined and its frequency noted. Establishing the frequency helps parents and pastor realistically understand the extent of the problem and offers a baseline by which to measure the effectiveness of any subsequent interventions. This is important in order to determine whether a specific brief pastoral counseling approach is working or whether other methods need to be initiated.

The assessment process first means defining the problem behavior in terms of its excesses (for undesirable activities) or deficiencies (for desirable actions), and then counting the number of times each problem occurs in a given period and recording that data on a chart. Measuring should be done over three or four days at a minimum, both when establishing a baseline and later during the counseling process. Also, it needs to be done at the same time each day, and for a specific length of time, since the occurrence of the problem may vary according to the child's or family's schedule.

For example, Ben beats up on his sister: a problem that needs resolution. Each day, his mother notes on a chart the number of times Ben antagonizes his sister from the moment he gets home from school until the family sits down for dinner. This two- to three-hour chart is kept for five consecutive days. In another situation, if an action occurs much more frequently than Ben's, a chart based on only an hour a day may suffice. If it occurs infrequently, the time frame for measurement may have to be a full day.

Involving both parents in counting the incidents (taking turns) is best. Also, charting their own related behaviors (such as how many positive reinforcers they have offered Ben or how often they have reprimanded him) can be helpful. This broadens the focus beyond the child's problem behavior to include the parents' reinforcement of undesirable actions or their failure to cue and reinforce the desired ones.

After the assessment process is well advanced, parents are taught the principles of reinforcement. Persuasiveness may be required on the part of the pastor to help them see that they (not the minister) are the agents of change and that improvement in the child's actions will depend upon them. Parents often want to deposit a problem child at the church's doorstep, thinking that because it is one of the last institutions concerned with what is good and right, the church will accomplish what they themselves have been unable to do: make their child behave. Parents learning the principles of reinforcement in relation to their children need education and motivation to see change as a possibility for themselves.

If the parents agree to the change process, then the next step is for them to refine their definition of the child's problem, being more specific than before and perhaps altering their definition as they observe it more carefully. Next they develop a plan of change, systematically introducing the new ways of acting to the child and practicing them with the child.

In brief pastoral counseling, the pastor's task is to help the parents choose humane goals for the child by pointing out instances in which they unwittingly pass on to the child the "sins" of their own childhoods. As consultant, the pastor is to coach the parents in their work toward change, helping them to hone their change-producing skills and encouraging them to persevere. Parents frequently do not do well at first, but even a little success will increase their motivation and confidence. Behavioral rehearsal (see chap. 7) can be used with the parents by having them practice their interaction with the child in the office before they return home and use their newly learned principles there.

Once change has begun to occur, both child and parents will be encouraged by their success. Parents are urged to make other changes in the parent-child relationship that are based not on catching the child being bad, but on rewarding the constructive behaviors and doing together things that are emotionally nourishing for everyone.

With the advent of change in a child's actions, I often ask parents if they want to apply the principles they have learned to some problem of their own. For example, if the parents are in debt, they may wish to use reinforcement methods to change their own spending habits. The child, observing the parents working responsibly toward a solution to their grown-up predicaments, will be further encouraged to learn new and more constructive behaviors. The principles of reinforcement are not just brief pastoral counseling methods for children: they can work for everyone.

6
Powerful Fears
∽
Imagery Approaches

Images are like magic. No matter where I am or what I am doing, I can close my eyes and summon a picture of the lake home in northern Minnesota where we spend our summers. I can see the cabin and look out through the pines to the lake. Bald eagles fly overhead and loons cry in alarm. Beavers busy themselves gathering food. I can see fishing boats anchored below the bank and watch storms move across the sky. I do not need to be at the cabin and the lake to feel the sun's warmth on my skin and catch the subtle scent of dry pine needles on the ground. Imagery can transport me to that place where I cannot be.

Images shape our lives. Imagine, for example, Janis, a writer who saw the face of her recently deceased husband every time she looked at a piece of blank paper. Understandably, she was paralyzed by this image, this emptiness, this loss. She could not write until several years later, when she could look again at a piece of paper without seeing his image.

Clearly, images can cause many emotional problems, but they also can heal. As Arnold Lazarus (1977, 39) notes, "Many professionals remain unaware that the deliberate and concerted use of specific images often proves to be the key that unlocks and opens the way to solve hitherto puzzling problems. Imagery opens up one of the most powerful areas of personality for overcoming innumerable daily stresses."

Neurosurgeon Wilder Penfield discovered that by electrically stimulating certain parts of the brain, patients hear or see past events from their lives. If he stimulated different parts of the brain, different images were recalled. Repeated stimulation of the same spot on the brain elicited the same memory.

Our brains store images of past events much like a motion picture library stores films. These accumulated images in the brain's library reappear to comfort or terrorize us, like the image of the lake cabin or the face of the deceased spouse staring from the writer's empty page. Negative images bind us with fear; positive images unleash the natural strength and health within us.

Images can even influence the physical performance of a task, as in a case I encountered at a pastoral counseling center in Arizona. Sunshine seems to attract baseball, and the Phoenix area is a spring training ground for many big league teams. As a pastoral counselor there, I saw many professional athletes—from Hall of Fame candidates to minor league hopefuls. In these athletes, I began to recognize the power of imagery for good or ill and its usefulness to brief pastoral counseling.

Randall was a young left-handed pitcher. He had a fast ball that left batters blinking and a curve that moved them off the plate. He also had a problem with control which doomed him to a life of obscurity in A and AAA ball. When he was relaxed in the bullpen and had no one watching, he had almost perfect control. Under stress, however, he lost command of his pitches. Sometimes he was completely wild, walking batter after batter until the manager pulled him from the mound. He was especially nervous before a crowd— an obvious drawback for a major league hopeful. Everyone agreed that he had the talent for the major leagues and might be there already if it were not for his control problem. Randall's coaches were frustrated with his wasted talent. In a moment of exasperation one of them said, "Why don't you see someone about your problem?" Randall took the advice; he went to a local minister who referred him to me.

I used several interventions to help Randall address his control problem, most of them focusing on imagery. I first used progressive relaxation exercises (see chap. 11), which helped but were not sufficient. Next, I used *coping imagery*. Randall closed his eyes and imagined the troubling situation (pitching in front of a large crowd with the bases full) and then imagined coping successfully with it (getting the ball low and in the strike zone). As vividly as possible he imagined himself working his way out of the jam, handling the situation realistically and with little anxiety. He ended each coping visualization with a relaxing image (lying in the sun on the beach). He practiced these images twice a day for ten or fifteen minutes each time.

Another imagery method, *goal rehearsal*, improved Randall's concentration. He pictured each one of his pitches from his first grasping of the ball to the ball entering the catcher's mitt. In slow motion he visualized the harmony of his body working to deliver the ball. He imaged—visualized in his mind—how he would pitch to different types of hitters, and, as he got to know certain players, the specific pitches needed to strike them out. Practicing this imagery technique every day was essential.

The coping imagery was the most useful of the interventions used in Randall's situation. He needed to relax, but most of all he needed to face his fear of being in a tough spot with hundreds of people watching, many of them hoping he would fail. It took some prodding on my part to get him to practice the imaging at home, but when I told him I was convinced he would never make it to the major leagues unless he conquered his fears, he practiced them. And he made it.

The use of imagery in religion is not new. Most faiths use images to make concrete what is abstract, transcendent, difficult to comprehend, or impossible to express through language. Images help people to actualize the goals of their faith. The Hebrew Bible is replete with imagery, visions, and visionary dreams: Lot's wife turning into a pillar of salt, the burning bush, seven fat cows devoured by seven lean ones. Kabbalah, the mystical tradition of Judaism, uses image, symbol, and visualization in its practice.

Imagery is also prominent in the tradition of Christian spirituality and spiritual direction (Stone 1988). Liturgical rites such as the Eucharist rely upon imagery: visualizing Christ offering the bread and wine to the disciples, making the Last Supper concrete. Another time and place is somehow united with our time and place, so that believers are united with the Christ and Christ's healing acts in this imaged event.

The field of psychotherapy and counseling has also used imagery in its practice. Freud discovered that patients who had relaxed through the use of hypnosis or other means could recall long-forgotten images from childhood. To a greater extent than Freud, Jung emphasized images and their importance for therapy. Both Freud and Jung learned that helping people to visualize emotionally charged events from their past diminished their disturbance. Freud stated that "it is possible for thought processes to become conscious through a reversion to visual residues. Thinking in pictures . . . approximates more closely to unconscious processes than does thinking in words, and is unquestionably older than the latter both ontogenetically and phylogenetically" (Samuels and Samuels 1975, 182).

Recently the French, Germans, and Italians have furthered the utilization of imagery in therapy. Many have extended Jung's understanding of the "active imagination" in which counselees re-dream certain dreams and re-experience past events through imagery. The United States also has witnessed a resurgence of interest in imagery for psychotherapy. Behaviorists have used it for systematic desensitization and flooding techniques, gestalt therapy has employed guided daydreams and dream extension, and the cognitive therapists capitalize on imagery to rehearse troubling events helping counselees catch their cognitive distortions. Many other schools of psychotherapy have discovered the power that resides in images and employ imagery in counseling.

This chapter will focus on how past and present images can aid counselees to cope with future difficulties. It is not a treatise on the hidden powers of the mind but rather a series of brief pastoral counseling interventions, most of which can be used as homework assignments (see chap. 2), which help people gain greater control over themselves and their problems.

THE USE OF IMAGERY

"Image," when used as a verb ("to image") in this chapter, refers to the act of visualizing some past or future event. Virtually everyone who is willing to relax and spend time is able to image. Even though wide differences in individuals' natural talent for visualization exist, the exercises assume only a rudimentary ability to form fairly clear images.

Lazarus (1977, 9–11) developed an imagery vividness scale that measures how well people are able to form images. In my experience, however, the simple act of listening to counselees reveals how well they see things in their minds and supplies all the information needed to determine if they are forming clear enough images to benefit from imagery techniques.

An initial visualization that is easy for most people to do is to picture a place from childhood. (Even though this is not a self-help book with exercises for readers, you may wish to close your eyes and try imaging several of the scenes in this and the following exercises.) Encourage counselees to close their eyes and see themselves in a room they recall. Suggest that they scan the room, discovering toys, furniture, pictures on the wall, windows, curtains, books, the floor. Ask them to open the door to a closet and peer inside, looking for prized possessions from the past. Prompt them to notice the colors, textures, and even smells if their image is that vivid. This simple visualization eases people's uncertainties about imaging and also reveals their aptitude to form images.

"The meadow" is another elementary image that can determine counselees' ability to visualize. (You may want to try it now yourself.) The pastor might say:

> Close your eyes, take a few deep breaths, and imagine yourself entering a large meadow. Go into it at your own pace. See the sky, the trees and grasses, feel the sun baking on your skin and the breeze blowing. Hear the sounds of the meadow. Do whatever you wish while you are in the meadow. I will leave you there for a brief time; let whatever happens take place. (Pause) Now leave the meadow at your own pace, slowly stretch your arms and legs, and open your eyes.

For most people (but not all) such an image is a relaxing, freeing experience. For once in their lives, they can do whatever they want or do nothing at all, and at their own pace.

After counselees finish the visualization, ask them to describe in detail what they saw, did, and felt. It can assist the helper's assessment of counselees' abilities to image and also gives some insights about their personalities.

Some people do not visualize successfully because they do not take the time to allow their minds to wander. When people permit themselves the time, the images residing within them bubble up to the surface. Horowitz (Samuels and Samuels 1975, 136) suggests that the ability to visualize increases when "planfulness decreases and persons enter a state of directionless thought."

Relaxation is another key to successful visualization. Many—possibly most—people who have difficulty visualizing are limited by their inability to relax. The clarity of images can be heightened by relaxation exercises; in fact, most of the imagery techniques described in this chapter should be preceded by some form of relaxation exercise—a few deep breaths or even just focusing upon one's breathing, if nothing else.

Imagery also can substitute for relaxation methods (described in chap. 11). Some counselees find relaxation exercises uninspiring and would rather employ imaging to calm themselves. They can close their eyes and imagine themselves in a relaxing situation, a sort of a mental mini-vacation. It may be a sandy beach or a forest walk, a long soak in a tub or a sunset. Counselees choose which images are most calming and mentally go to them for a few minutes whenever they feel overtaken by anxiety.

A great advantage of such visualization is that it often enables people to slip around verbal roadblocks. Counselees who use words as defenses are prime candidates for imaging because images pierce with clarity through their verbiage. Imaging techniques are essential for counselees who are ministers or university professors who often are masters of word manipulation, but are also potentially confused by them. Ask them to refrain from analyzing, but simply to let the images speak for themselves. Words powerfully convey meaning but also distort it. Images can break through language to truth.

To heighten visualization, I sometimes employ one of two methods—*zoom* and *slow motion*—both analogous to cameras. I will ask counselees to zoom in on a particular detail (e.g., a daughter explaining a failing grade on a report card) to help them see it more clearly and in greater detail. Those who image the practice of a particular task (e.g., the baseball pitcher's curve ball) visualize the activity like a *slow motion* camera, noting every aspect of what they are doing. Both methods supply greater detail to the image.

A comment regarding children: Most parents have run to the room of a screaming toddler to find the child frightened by a nightmare or an imaginary goblin. Children live in a world of images that are more basic and vivid than those of adults. Sometimes they can bring out the images that haunt them by drawing pictures. Another direct way of getting at images that terrorize children is reading stories related to their fears or having them make up stories about imaginary boys or girls facing similar situations. Each of these can help them express their fears.

IMAGERY TECHNIQUES

Imagery interventions for counseling abound and continue to be developed by the many schools of psychotherapy that have adopted them. Spiritual direction provides even more methods of using imagery. Below are several imagery techniques that are suited to brief pastoral counseling and address some of the more common problems encountered in parish ministry.

Accomplishment Rehearsal

Chris Evert, one of my tennis heroes, makes good use of accomplishment rehearsal. Many other athletes and people in a wide variety of pursuits also use accomplishment rehearsal well, often without knowing they are doing it. Evert thinks about her opponent's strengths and weaknesses and style of play. She rehearses in her mind how she will counter each of her challenger's shots, imaging her own returns. She imagines herself combating each of her challenger's strokes before ever reaching the court.

Lazarus (1977, 67) cites another example from sports:

> If a golfer imagines himself driving a ball or making a difficult putt over and over again, his actual game will improve. Similarly, the mental practice of picturing oneself successfully throwing darts at a target will improve one's aim in the real situation. This applies to nearly all specific skills. If you practice something in imagination, it is bound to have an effect on the real situation.

Countless skills can be polished using this technique: a shy person greeting people at work; a compliant wife asserting herself with her husband; a businessperson speaking in front of a crowd of people; a minister saying "no" to a certain church member; a boss greeting employees in a friendly manner; and many other attitudes, skills, and traits.

Counselees need to learn specifically what is required in order to perform a certain skill—such as precisely what "being friendly to employees" means (smiling at each one, saying hello, asking about their families, complimenting them on their work, and so forth). If an endeavor is complex, then discuss how each of the actions fit together. Counselees must know how to perform a task in all of its particulars before they can image it.

When counselees have difficulty acting in a desired way, sometimes it is good to have them exaggerate the behavior in their imaging. A shy man may greet others effusively, for instance, or an underconfident woman may assert herself with her husband in things that do not matter to her.

When people want to change something in their lives, they accomplish it best by first visualizing it in their imagination. The effectiveness of accomplishment rehearsal cannot be overstated; imagination is a key to implementing brief pastoral counseling goals. Counselees can practice it as a homework task.

A Spiritual Direction Exercise

Spiritual direction heightens and strengthens people's awareness of God's presence. "[It] is concerned with awareness of and growth in one's relationship with God. It has reference to a place—a person, actually—where Christians can go to talk specifically about that relationship. It suggests a method of pastoral care that sensitizes people to that presence of God that already exists, in which we live" (Stone 1988, 94).

Many disciplines, methods, or exercises are used in connection with spiritual direction to facilitate openness to God. Prayer, contemplation, journals, Scripture, and meditation serve that objective and can be a fruitful resource for developing a contemplative attitude and for paying attention to one's own inner experience of the divine. Neither the relationship of spiritual direction to brief pastoral counseling nor the practice of spiritual direction can be covered here. (See Stone 1988; Barry and Connolly 1983.) In relating such direction to imagery in brief pastoral counseling, at least one exercise from the spiritual disciplines bears discussing.

Imagery has long been a part of spiritual exercises intended to heighten one's relationship with God. One way imagery is used in spiritual direction has been to tie it to Scripture. For example, after practicing some preparatory quieting exercises (relaxation training, monologia, and so forth), counselees may be asked to form an image of a biblical scene in their mind's eye. After reading the Scripture passage several times, they close their eyes and, using their eyelids as a screen, visualize themselves as part of the story—as Zacchaeus up in the tree, perhaps, or as a lamb beside the still waters. They try to picture everything as vividly as possible, smelling the smells, hearing the sounds, tasting the food and drink. They do not have to move the story's characters around as a stage director would move them, but should participate with a receptive attitude and let whatever happens happen. Counselees may permit themselves to say or do things that are not precisely described in the passage.

Such an endeavor allows Scripture to come alive. For those who have difficulty apprehending the healing that Christ offered to the leper, the forgiveness given to the woman by the well, the salvation revealed to Paul on the road to Damascus, imaging can be a powerful way to participate in the event as if it were happening. It also can help them to receive what has already been given, but often is hard to sense. It can have an intense impact for some women who feel disenfranchised by a male-dominated religion; visualizing the women at the cross or at the tomb, for example, may allow them to feel a part of the drama of salvation. Psalms, parables, and narrative sections of the Gospels are especially suitable for imaging. Having initially visualized a passage in this way, individuals can return to the same image repeatedly, allowing it to continue speaking to them.

Systematic Desensitization

Applied appropriately and with care, systematic desensitization is not difficult to master. Its components include the following: (1) relaxing (sometimes omitted), (2) explaining the method to the counselee, (3) developing a hierarchical list of troubling events, and (4) imaging. To illustrate these components as they function in a counseling situation, let me share a case which, although unusual, provides a good illustration of how systematic desensitization works.

Connie was a forty-six-year-old real estate agent. Even though she was married, she saw little of her husband, who was a computer consultant and traveled extensively. Connie had a problem with a particular fear: She had been visiting a psychotherapist for six months, and before that, a hypnotist, without results. Her fear was that in public situations, she would have an intense urge to urinate and would find it awkward or difficult to extricate herself from her clients while meeting in her office or showing a home.

She urinated two or three times an hour as a routine precaution so that if someone came into her presence, she would not be embarrassed by having to excuse herself to go to the bathroom. She sometimes urinated as many as fifty times a day. She made a point of never leaving home or the office for more than half an hour at a time—an awkward limitation in the real estate business. Connie always urinated before going out with prospective customers and before appointments in her office. The first thing she did when she reached any destination was to scout out the restroom. Because of her fear, Connie had almost stopped going to church, movies, and concerts and flying in airplanes; she felt as if every eye was on her whenever she headed for the toilet.

Although a medical check-up ruled out physical causes for Connie's condition, careful psychological assessment disclosed no major traumatic event that could be identified as the cause of the phobia. Her condition had developed gradually over the previous two to three years. Previous counseling also had found no trauma, but had discovered a tentative relationship between her husband's travels and her difficulties.

Systematic desensitization often is beneficial in relieving such fears and phobias—situations in which anxiety is conditioned, yet there is actually no significant danger. These phobias include the fear of flying, cramped places, examinations, crowds, being watched by others, talking before large groups of people, heights, and so forth.

After assessment, Connie's pastor taught her a few relaxation techniques. During her relaxation training, the pastor decided to use systematic desensitization. Desensitization, Connie learned, is based on the premise that an image can functionally represent a real-life situation. Therefore, once she could learn to "image" being in a public place for several hours without any concern or anxiety about urinating, she would be able to duplicate the experience in real life.

Connie and her pastor developed a list of troublesome events, using his notes about her history and her own enumeration of possible items. Her husband also was asked to help. At the next session the lengthy list was pruned to seventeen items, which Connie ranked according to the amount of anxiety they caused. The result was Connie's hierarchical list of troubling events and situations: one, a long plane trip in the window seat on which she felt a strong urge to urinate; two, a long car trip where she would have to request others to stop the car so she can urinate; and so forth on down to number sixteen—at home with her husband, watching TV; and the least troubling situation, number seventeen, was eating a bowl of ice cream in the kitchen when no one else is home.

After Connie had learned to relax, had learned the concept of systematic desensitization, and had ranked her list of troublesome events, her desensitization procedure began. At the beginning of each counseling session, Connie practiced relaxation exercises for five minutes. While she was relaxing with her eyes closed, the pastor described item number seventeen from the list using as many details as possible to make it come alive. The pastor urged Connie to imagine additional particulars to make the situation as graphic as possible: the room where the scene took place, the arrangements of the furniture, even tastes or smells if they could help her capture the experience and make her feel as if she were really there.

In systematic desensitization, after the image has been described and imaged, the attendant feelings need to be assessed and identified. The helper says, "If the imaging triggers even the slightest anxiety or fear, raise your left index finger. If none, then do nothing."

Connie had little trouble learning to image. Each scene was presented for five to thirty seconds (less if she appeared uncomfortable). After each presentation she was told, "Banish the scene from your mind and just relax. Feel yourself calm and relaxed." After a fifteen to forty-five second pause the scene was presented again. When Connie could image the situation several times without any feeling of disturbance, the next highest item in the hierarchy was introduced.

Connie had little trouble with the bottom items on her list. Most of the counseling time (five sessions) was spent on the middle situations. By the time she arrived at the final items, they moved fairly quickly and, because of her practiced skill in imaging, triggered little anxiety. When they reached the top-ranked item, a long-distance flight, however, Connie and her pastor used a procedure known as "flooding." Together they created the most anxious scene they could conjure, and she was asked to visualize it—realizing that she would have some anxiety, but knowing that she could handle it. The scene she chose was flying on a ten-hour transatlantic flight so rough that the "fasten seat belt" sign remained lit almost the entire trip. She experienced some anxiety, but was not greatly troubled by it, having learned through much practice that she could live with a measure of anxiety and not panic. Systematic desensitization enabled her to visualize all the items in her list by moving through them gradually without appreciable distress. Systematic desensitization relieves the anxiety and fears counselees experience. When they are able to visualize scenes in their minds without appreciable anxiety, they are able to experience events in real life without the distress they had prior to using it.

Self-control Imagery

Marvin Goldfried (1971) developed a variation of systematic desensitization using self-control. In traditional systematic desensitization, a scene is presented in its entirety for the counselee, with the aim of reducing the person's anxiety about that situation. In the self-control variation, a setting with inherent anxiety is introduced, but the counselee is urged, even while imaging, to resolve the situation and bring it to completion. By taking responsibility for the solution as well as for conquering anxiety, the person is less dependent upon the helper and is taught to cope, in the words of Goldfried, "with anxiety responses and cues rather than with situations which elicit the tension" (230).

Self-control imagery is geared to overcoming phobias and fears (the approach used with Randall, the pitcher afraid of performing before a crowd). Counselees ask themselves precisely what is necessary for them to cope with the fearful situation. After discussing it with the helper, they image the predicament, seeing the scene clearly (some people want to avoid this), and face any unpleasant feelings it may arouse. Next they visualize themselves handling the situation, bringing it to some sort of resolution with little or no distress.

For example, Manuel, a forty-seven-year-old single man, was afraid to date, but wanted to ask a coworker out for dinner. He is presented with the imaginary scene of standing by the woman's desk and wanting to ask her for dinner that evening. He imagines the end of the scene, deciding what would happen next, and brings the situation to a resolution.

The regular practice of self-control imagery helps counselees to replace negative images of anxiety and failure with confident images of coping well in difficult areas of life. When people address these difficulties in real life, they find that they can do the things they had feared.

Assessment Imagery

Images may also benefit the assessment process in brief pastoral counseling. They can trace the source of recurring disturbances to help determine the source of continually troublesome events. In particular, images that are associated with depression, anxiety, frustration, and anger sometimes pinpoint the basis of the disturbance.

To use imagery for assessment, counselees first relax and close their eyes. They then talk about the feelings that haunt them. Next they amplify their negative feelings. If depressed, for example, they deepen their disposition until they are really down. Once they feel the negative emotions strongly, they try to become aware of any images that may rise to the surface. Whatever images they are, counselees visualize them as intensely and graphically as possible. As additional images appear, they try to see them as vividly as the others. With their eyes closed as they view the scenes, they relate in the first person everything they see ("now I see . . ."). Certain images may require special attention in order to draw out the details; the slow motion or zoom techniques mentioned previously sometimes serve well here. Finally, counselees have the chance to explore the feelings associated with their images, thus actively participating in their assessment process.

Images can pierce the screen of words and reveal the core of a problem. For this reason they benefit assessment in brief pastoral counseling, and can hasten understanding and accelerate the care process.

Fire Drill Imagery

Most of us as children practiced fire drills in school. The drills prepared us to act safely and calmly in the event of a real fire. Fire drill imagery helps people prepare for unpredictable calamities in their lives. It is a way to emotionally rehearse and plan what they will do in the event of misfortune.

When I raced a stock car years ago, I often mentally practiced what I would do if something bad happened to me: if I rolled, if the car caught fire, if the throttle stuck open, and so forth. One of the worst scenarios in stock car racing is to spin out with the car ending up perpendicular to the track with the driver's door facing the oncoming cars. This position allows the car to be "T-boned," that is, hit in the driver's door, a vulnerable spot even with a full roll cage surrounding the driver.

One Friday night, I broke an axle, lost a wheel, and spun out at the end of the back straightaway. Immediately I knew that my car could be T-boned. Many times I had imaged myself leaning toward the center of the car and grasping one of the pipes that make up the roll cage. The inevitable happened: I was hit at the driver's door by a car traveling seventy-five miles per hour. The driver never saw me. There was no time to think, but in the microsecond before he hit me, I knew what was going to happen. I instinctively leaned over and grasped the center of the cage just as I had imaged it. The scene in my mind came to life exactly as planned, and I suffered only a few bumps and bruises to show for it.

Crisis theorists (Stone 1993) note that when confronted with major situational crises, most people initially have difficulty coping with the misfortune. They freeze up, and if they act at all, fail to engage in purposeful activities which would remedy the problem. People in crisis also tend to have tunnel vision and find it difficult to sort out their options. Often they exhibit rigid thinking and considerable anxiety.

Fire drill rehearsal (Lazarus 1977) lets people plan ahead for potentially challenging events. I have found it useful in many situations, such as a husband who may soon be divorced: parents facing the empty nest; a wife whose husband has inoperable cancer; a person who once attempted suicide and will likely feel suicidal again; a student applying for graduate school who may not get in; a graduate student in English who may not be hired for the full-time university teaching position she desires; a man who may be laid off or fired from his job.

Fire drill imagery asks counselees to relax, close their eyes, and visualize the possible occurrence. The engineer in his fifties who senses he may be edged out of his position and maybe even his job imagines it happening in vivid detail. His focus is not on the younger employees who may have his job, but on what he will do if he is out of work. He visualizes the specific steps he will take to determine if he can get back his job or get another job: writing resumes, interviewing for jobs, contacting colleagues in the field who can help him, and so forth. He images friends who can encourage him and family who can provide support. The imagery should be as concrete as possible and the actions he takes as specific as he can make them.

To avert the paralysis and rigid thinking that occur in a crisis, fire drill imagery allows individuals to picture ways they could handle a significant crisis should it occur. Unfortunately many individuals do not think through these events clearly or visualize in detail what may lie ahead and thus suffer from their shortsighted decisions and hasty actions.

The use of imagery in counseling will continue to grow. Its power is only beginning to come to the fore, even though Christian mystics and spiritual directors have known about it for centuries. It is dynamic and, like behavioral rehearsal, helps people move from thinking about a problem to doing something to challenge it. Imaging is tailored for brief pastoral counseling; it hastens the counseling process, helping people more rapidly to "see" their problems and address them.

7

Difficult Changes

$\backsim$

Behavioral Rehearsal

Change is the goal, the end, the purpose, the *telos* of brief pastoral counseling. When change does not take place, the reasons usually given are that the counselee was insufficiently motivated, resistant, and unwilling to risk the steps necessary for the change to occur. This is most likely true, but there is more to the story. People often do not achieve the desired change because it seems so far beyond their reach that fear or anxiety takes over. They also do not know how to do what needs to be done: they lack the needed skills.

In brief pastoral counseling, the minister needs to make change seem readily possible and help counselees acquire the skills needed to accomplish their goals. Many times knowing what needs to change is not enough. *Insight does not necessarily lead to action!* Something must come between the knowledge about the needed change and the change itself. This task between thought and action is central to brief pastoral counseling, and if it is left out of the change process, the counselee is sometimes mistakenly thought to be under-motivated.

For example, the pastor may ask a husband to express his feelings to his wife—a husband who spends all of his time in an occupation where the overt expression of emotion is actively discouraged so that he hardly knows what a feeling is. The man most likely will not express his feelings to his wife not because of lack of motivation, but because of lack of skill.

How can people be helped to do what they know needs to be done? Several options are available for the pastoral counselor. Relaxation training (chap. 11) is helpful for those who are bullied by worry or apprehension. Teaching communication skills, emotional expression, or reinforcement principles is especially useful for those who lack the skills to deal with their problems. Behavioral rehearsal can also encourage people to do what they need to do by helping them reduce anxiety, face fears, and develop the skills needed for change.

BEHAVIORAL REHEARSAL

For change to occur in a person's life, a transitional step is needed between knowing and doing. Behavioral rehearsal, otherwise known as role playing, used as an approach to simulating interpersonal situations, goes back as far as the early 1800s (Ziboorg and Henry 1941).

I began employing behavioral rehearsal during my training as a pastoral counselor. A supervisor remarked that my counseling was sound, but lacked finesse. Whenever I felt change would be beneficial in the counseling process, I would abruptly say, "I think you need to do _____ ." Counselees often agreed, but would then stare forward as though on a diving board, trembling, unwilling to take the leap. I would then quickly retreat and try to coerce, cajole, plead, or beg, but by that time resistance had built up, fears developed, and the person refused to participate.

Using behavioral rehearsal in counseling requires subtlety and tact. The counselee first needs conviction that learning the new activity is worthwhile. This is important. Jumping from assessing a junior executive's problem to behavioral rehearsal involving assertiveness with the boss will doom the learning process to failure unless the junior executive learns and believes the potential benefits of being assertive with the employer.

Once convinced of the value of the desired behavior, the technique of behavioral rehearsal should be explained. As much as possible, allow the subject to come up naturally in the conversation. Describe behavioral rehearsal as a dry run, much like practicing a speech in front of a mirror or trying a golf swing without a ball. Relate how it has been helpful with previous counselees, citing someone who had difficulty "getting into" behavioral rehearsal at first, but who eventually found it worthwhile. Tell counselees that in behavioral rehearsal, you expect they will be awkward in the beginning and will not say all the right things, but that it is better that they practice here, where it doesn't count than out in the world where it does.

Deal with the counselee's resistance. Resistance to behavioral rehearsal can be great, so preparations are necessary unless a counselee has previously used the procedure with a measure of success. Some people refuse to believe that practicing in the pastor's office really can help. When a person remarks, "It's artificial," simply agree and

101

add, "Yes, it is artificial, but what you are learning and the feelings that result are real." For example, once, when training a group of pastors, two trainees were assigned the roles of husband and wife with marital problems. Even though they had not met previously, they developed such strong antipathy toward each other during behavioral rehearsal that they had to stay after class for half an hour of debriefing!

Next, encourage the person to role-play or rehearse. Frequently the new behavior is easily defined and requires little preparation beyond practicing it. A father can redo a parent-child fight in which he expelled his daughter from the house. In practice, he would start over again and try a different way of handling the disagreement, perhaps several different ways leading to quite different results.

USING BEHAVIORAL REHEARSAL

Below are suggestions for using behavioral rehearsal in brief pastoral counseling:

- Try to select scenes in which the counselees initiate action instead of being acted upon. For example, they initiate a conversation with someone they fear rather than waiting for that person to approach them. A basic tenet of brief pastoral counseling is that it is better for people to *initiate* the changes that they are trying to make than to wait for someone else to act upon them.

- If the desired change is complex or very troublesome, then develop and rank a list of scenes and begin rehearsing the easiest, moving toward the more difficult at a gradual pace so that the counselees are stretched without being made too uncomfortable.

- Individuals who are new to behavioral rehearsal often benefit from trying "warm-up" scenes which pose no threat. Learning rehearsal methods often eases the stage fright and uncertainties they may otherwise feel.

- Use as many details as necessary to make the scenes vivid. Instruct people who are redoing a troublesome past event to use the same situational background in a fresh way, not re-playing the scene but approaching it as if it never happened before.

■ Urge counselees to stay within the scene even if they become afraid or want to flee. Have them express their fears and then rethink the situation in fresh scenarios until they are not so intimidated. Sometimes cognitive restructuring can be used to address the fears.

■ It is better that the pastor does not play a part in behavioral rehearsal scenes. This makes the pastor available to coach coun-selees while they act out their roles. Unfortunately, unless the counselee is in a group session or has family members along, the pastor is often cast in a role by default. If the minister is in the scene, the minister should move to another chair to say symbolically that he or she is taking a new part for the moment. When playing the part of a particularly disagreeable character, the minister should move back to his or her former chair and say something like: "Whew! I'm glad I don't have to play him [or her] anymore!"

■ Sometimes people do not make changes simply because they do not know where to begin. At such times, modeling or demonstrating the desired behavior is helpful. In demonstrating a new approach or style, the caregiver should offer specifics on how to act differently. I occasionally attempt to model for one spouse alternative ways of treating the other. One might try it with those who are seeking a job, but are having a difficult time getting one. The caregiver should help them see how they can act while being interviewed by a personnel officer.

■ Be ready to move to relaxation exercises when anxiety be-comes too great, either beforehand or in the middle of a scene. (Use the relaxation methods described in chapter 11 before proceeding with the rehearsal.)

■ Practice a scene for a short period of time; do not allow scenes to go on for more than a few minutes. It is better to practice a scene several times than to do one long one. (Scenes of five to ten minutes are useful after a series of shorter scenes; the longer scene puts all of the lessons together into a more complex unit.) The first few attempts at behavioral rehearsal may last only a minute or two.

■ Try role reversal, such as when husband plays wife and vice versa or mother plays daughter and vice versa. Role reversal can have a surprising effect. Although this does not give clients practice in a new behavior, they gain awareness of each other's feelings and how difficult it is to be that person. This technique often breaks down the adversarial relationships that sometimes overtake families.

After a scene has been practiced, two things remain: First, talk with the counselee about how well it was played and elicit suggestions for improvement. Second, clarify how the lessons will be transferred into daily life. Because the purpose of behavioral rehearsal is to assist counselees in putting into action what they have learned in counseling, ask how much of what they did in behavioral rehearsal will be used in daily life. This becomes a homework assignment for the coming week.

Behavioral rehearsal is a useful way to try, in the safety of the pastor's office, what may be a frightening experience outside. Behavioral rehearsal is especially suited to situations such as being assertive, applying for a job, giving speeches, and meeting people in public. It also is helpful in family relationships for practicing new ways of relating.

Individuals who are poorly socialized—that is, in the process of maturation, who did not pick up the commonly accepted attitudes, mores, and interpersonal skills that allow them to function effectively among other people—are helped by behavioral rehearsal. Behavioral rehearsal can encourage those who lack such skills to develop what most people take for granted. For example, I use it to help shy or withdrawn adolescents or young adults in their dating relationships.

People are much more likely to do in real life what they talk about in the session if behavioral rehearsal has been practiced first. As a result, behavioral rehearsal is a prominent intervention for brief pastoral counseling.

8

Obsessive Thoughts

∽

Thought Mastery Procedures

One sunny afternoon in the early fall fifty-three-year-old Jessica Walters was taking care of her four-year-old grandson Ricky. Hearing the screech of brakes in front of her house, she rushed outside to see Ricky sprawled on the pavement next to the twisted remains of his tricycle.

After five days in the hospital and two weeks convalescing at home, Ricky seemed fully recovered. Jessica, however, was not so lucky. She had trouble sleeping and eating, and from morning to night she chastised herself for being the cause of Ricky's accident. In the past when Ricky had visited her house and asked to go outside, she had said "Ricky, you be careful and don't play in the street." But on the day of the accident she had gone upstairs for a moment. When she returned, he was already outside playing. Not more than five minutes later, the car struck.

Two months later, Jessica's self-recrimination was still going on. Her son and daughter-in-law had forgiven her, and Ricky had no after-effects except a little more respect for motor vehicles, yet she continued to replay the event in her mind. Finally, Ricky's mother suggested that Jessica see her pastor.

THOUGHT STOPPING

Jerry Charles knew the events well, having visited the child and his parents in the hospital several times. At first Pastor Charles tried to play down Jessica's problem, but soon he recognized that her distress was not abating. Together he and Jessica explored her feelings. This brought understanding and insight, and Jessica agreed that there was no reason for her to continue feeling guilty, but her obsessive memories of the accident continued.

Pastor Charles then made a decision to use a brief pastoral counseling intervention commonly called *thought stopping*, which is a mode of treatment for anxious individuals who have obsessive, ruminative thoughts they are unable to dispel.

After explaining the procedure to Jessica, the pastor had her sit back in a chair, close her eyes, and relax. He then asked her to think of and visualize eating from a bowl of fruit, an image that posed no threat. She was to indicate by raising her left index finger when she had fully developed the image. As soon as she did, Pastor Charles yelled "Stop!"

Thus began Jessica's practice of thought stopping. They repeated the procedure four or five times and took a few more practice runs with other innocuous images. After Jessica began to feel comfortable with the method, Pastor Charles told her to bring to mind her obsessive thought about Ricky. She indicated the thought by raising her left index finger, and again he barked "Stop!"

It is impossible to think of two very different things at the same time. For one moment at least, the obsessive thought is banished by the shout, "Stop!" After each presentation Pastor Charles asked Jessica if the thought had disappeared, if only for a short time. When she reported that it had, he responded, "Good. Each time this is practiced you will become better and better at being able to dispel your unwanted thoughts."

After a number of exchanges in which Pastor Charles yelled stop, he asked Jessica to shout it herself when she thought about the accident. After she was proficient at that and reported dispelling the unwanted thought, he instructed her to yell stop in her mind only, without saying anything out loud. In repeated exercises she alternated between saying stop vocally and saying it only in her mind. Eventually she became comfortable and assured in doing it either way. Finally, when she was able momentarily to dispel the obsessive thought at will, she was instructed to do it only subvocally.

Pastor Charles sent Jessica away that day with two homework assignments: First, she was to practice thought stopping for five minutes three times a day, purposely thinking about Ricky's accident and then banishing the thoughts with the thought-stopping procedure. Second, she was to use thought stopping every time she thought about the accident involuntarily.

When Jessica came in for a second session, Pastor Charles asked her how the thought stopping had gone. "Only fair," she reported, admitting that she was not sure it would help and that she did not practice much (a common response of counselees). To counselees, thought stopping seems magical, and most do not believe in magic.

Instead of scolding Jessica or abandoning the method, Pastor Charles repeated much of what he had done in the previous session, reinforcing it. He urged her to practice thought stopping again and told her of others (without using names or recognizable details) who had used it successfully. Jessica and Pastor Charles practiced thought stopping once more during the session, and he asked her if she had any questions.

At her third session, Jessica reported great success. Her ruminative thoughts had decreased considerably. She was able to banish the agonizing memories for longer and longer periods of time. Pastor Charles saw Jessica several times more to check on her progress with the thought stopping and to introduce ancillary counseling methods until her obsession lessened. (Thought stopping is usually more beneficial when used in conjunction with other counseling and anxiety-reduction interventions.)

Thought stopping is neither thought repression nor is it effective if used as such. To repress the thought is to drive it underground where it can fester and do greater emotional damage. To stop the thought is to face it, deal with it, and gradually master it.

Carla Moen, a young television producer, was working on a series of short documentaries for public television. Her colleague on the project was an older and more experienced woman. As their work advanced, duties multiplied and deadlines approached. Carla, ordinarily healthy, began to have symptoms of stress which included an upset stomach, insomnia, forgetfulness, reduction of her ability to think clearly, and obsessive thoughts about the money they had spent and the mountain of work ahead.

When her colleague left town for ten days on other business, the break in routine gave Carla time to assess her situation. She shared her trapped and anxious feelings with her minister, Pastor Alltop. Carla saw that she had been allowing her partner to dominate the relationship and push her into a project that was more ambitious and demanding than she wanted so early in her career. Her work was conflicting with other things that she valued in life: family, friends, and music (she was an accomplished violinist). While learning to be assertive in relation to her male colleagues, Carla had failed to assert her own wishes and goals with this female colleague whom she admired and respected.

With the help of Pastor Alltop's more dispassionate insights, Carla put her finger on the problem. She then decided that she must have a talk with her colleague, raise these issues, and make some changes in their partnership. She carefully listed the problems and possible solutions, and even wrote an agenda for the meeting with her co-producer.

But six days would pass before Carla could see her partner, and she was having trouble accomplishing some of her other day-to-day tasks. She repeatedly agonized about how she had been a doormat, rehearsed in her mind what she would say to the woman when the confrontation did finally occur, slept little, and felt physically exhausted.

Carla read a chapter from a book Pastor Alltop had given her about thought-stopping techniques. Lying awake and agitated at 2:00 A.M., she skipped over the first few steps and began silently yelling stop! to herself every time she thought about her project or her colleague or their upcoming confrontation. She was asleep in no time, helped by the thought-stopping method—but also by her belief that it would work. Because the procedure made sense to her, she showed none of Jessica's resistance to it.

Five days later Carla met with her collaborator and cleared the air. She was more rested and was relatively calm. Having reduced her obsessive thoughts about the meeting, she needed only a quick review of the agenda in order to be on top of the situation. Her colleague, as it turned out, had no desire to be so dominant in the relationship. She agreed willingly to the new ground rules Carla requested. Because they were both conflict avoiders by habit, they agreed in the future to bring up their disagreements immediately. The relationship was changed and both it and the television series was saved. Two weeks later Carla went back for some renegotiating. This time she was able to limit her future involvement in the project to a tolerable two months more.

If Carla had used thought repression, then her relationship with her colleague likely would have deteriorated to the point where it was past saving, and Carla's own emotional state probably would have been so shaky that she would have become physically ill. By using thought stopping, however, she faced her feelings and projected a solution to the problem. Thought stopping enabled Carla to lessen those thoughts that were useless to her during the interim. She was able to sleep, gain emotional distance from her work, and be at her best while negotiating the necessary changes in a professional relationship that she valued.

Carla's pastor, fortunately, recognized that she had both the intelligence and the motivation to solve her own problems and that all she needed from him was an objective viewpoint and some useful information. A mistake in any type of helping, and especially in brief pastoral counseling, is thinking that counselees are necessarily weak and helpless, unable to work actively for their own growth.

WRITE, READ, AND BURN

Pastors doing counseling commonly encounter recently divorced persons who cannot stop thinking about their past marriage relationship and the circumstances leading to its end. Benjamin Gold was one such individual. His thirteen-year marriage had ended in separation and then divorce. Night and day he could think of little else. His work was suffering, and a full night's sleep was infrequent.

Benjamin's minister told him that it is natural to give time to reflection after a divorce, and that a review of the relationship actually promotes the healing process. Such reflection, however, should not consume every moment of one's day. An intervention developed by de Shazer (1985), called "Write, Read, and Burn," was proposed.

Benjamin was instructed to set aside one hour, the same time each day, during which he would concentrate on the past marriage. On even-numbered days he would write down all his memories of the relationship, both good and bad. He was to write for the full hour, even if it meant rewriting the same few sentences over and over again. On odd-numbered days he would read the previous day's notes and then burn them. If his obsessive ruminations would crop up at other times, then Benjamin would instruct himself to delay the thought until the appointed hour. He was to repeat the even- and odd-day cycle until the obsessive thoughts abated.

"Write, Read, and Burn" needs to be presented to the counselee with conviction. Some individuals have difficulty believing that substituting thinking with writing and burning can serve any purpose. The minister's confidence in the intervention will facilitate counselees' willingness to participate. (A few people have difficulty burning what they write. The minister can urge them instead to keep their writings in a diary.)

This intervention works for several reasons: First, it objectifies counselees' concerns, making them more clear-cut and manageable. Second, it converts the "bad" thoughts from a taboo to a part of each day's tasks. Third, persons are less likely to dwell on them at other times during the day since a time is scheduled for them. Counselees eventually allow more important matters to come to the fore, and the obsessive ruminations decrease or disappear altogether.

"Write, Read, and Burn" is useful for obsessive thoughts of all sorts—not only those concerning divorce. Rarely do counselees need to use this intervention longer than a couple of weeks before the thoughts come under control. Along with thought stopping, this is a way ministers can help their counselees get control over thoughts that have become their master. Hopefully, too, they can get some sleep and redirect the wasted energy of obsessive thinking toward more productive pursuits.

9

Challenging Impasses
∽
Confrontation

Confrontation (the interpersonal method of choice in some circles) is in vogue and in recent years we have been encouraged to confront nearly everyone. Pastors confront parishioners and parishioners confront pastors; parents confront children and children confront parents; professors confront students and students confront their teachers; employers confront employees and employees confront employers.

At one extreme, much confrontation is little more than cynical and narcissistic venting of negative feelings. Unfortunately, instead of benefitting the relationship, it often demeans, shames, or belittles. Such confrontation arises from a condescending self-righteousness on the part of the confronter. The one who is in the know, with the correct beliefs or actions, supposedly helps the other.

At the other extreme, many people still withhold their own ideas or perspectives rather than impose them on others. Pastors in this camp may not want to be associated with the admittedly unfair stereotype of people with simple, easy answers to difficult questions (i.e., fundamentalists or arch-conservatives), and thus they say nothing. Can they be faulted for not wanting to give easy answers? After all, they simply do not want to impose their own beliefs on others. But they offer a stone to those who are hungry for bread, no words of faith for those seeking the bread of life.

When time is critical, as in brief pastoral counseling, confrontation can be a powerful tool in the hands of the pastor if it is used wisely. It can hasten the pace of the care offered. Ralph Underwood (1985, 95) puts it this way: "When pastors have parishioners' trust, their concerns can usually be explored readily so that pastors need not wait interminably, as if they were engaged in long-term therapy, before confronting. Consequently, empathy and confrontation can be placed together."

Confrontation assists people more rapidly in facing what needs to be faced and in doing what needs to be done. As a part of the prophetic or interpretative task of ministry, this task resides not only in social action, preaching, or teaching but also in pastoral counseling. Underwood (1985, 107) says that

> pastoral interpretation is the sharing of information and opinions about Christian truth that may assist persons in their celebration and conduct of life. It is spiritual and moral guidance in the inductive, not educative mode. . . . I do not believe that interpretation is reserved for corporate worship and the church's educational program. In fact, as Don Browning has explained, moral thinking is the task of the entire church and is an essential dimension of pastoral care.

Confrontation is an opportunity for individualized proclamation of the Word of God (Thurneysen, 1962), and helps persons develop a theological or ethical understanding of their own experience.

WOUNDED CONFRONTERS

The church of my youth used confrontation, although it did not use that term. The sins of others were major topics for discussion: sins such as going steady, dancing, kissing on the first date, wearing lipstick, and especially sex. Those who had fallen into sin often were confronted verbally. Such encounters tended to be as from the blameless to one entrenched in sin. They had a smug self-righteous tone about them.

This attitude is still found today, although more subtly, in mainline denominations where the focus is not so much on personal (especially sexual) sins as on social injustices or political correctness. If someone, for example, does not have the proper beliefs about animal rights, does not use inclusive language, does not show proper concern for the environment or nuclear disarmament, then confrontation may occur, frequently accompanied by the same smug self-righteous tone. The holier-than-thou attitude I experienced in my youth is still alive—it just dresses differently. (Not that the scrutiny of personal morality is a thing of the past. Many churches and secular groups are like my childhood church in this regard. Note how the press and public alike supervise politicians' personal lives.)

It is difficult to imagine any good resulting from self-righteous confrontation, but a different, more helpful sort of confrontation exists, informed by the thinking of Henry Nouwen. In his classic, *The Wounded Healer* (1979), Nouwen describes the helper as being little different from the one for whom care is offered. Both exist in sin; both have their own pain, alienation, and finitude. In ministry, while binding and unbinding the other's wounds, we are at the same time binding and unbinding our own wounds; while confronting the other we are being confronted. In this regard, both helper and the helped are of the same cloth.

Counseling respects the counselee and the counselee's worlds. Respect, when added to empathy, prevents confrontation from becoming self-righteous. Helpful confrontation also values persons and their world. We are wounded confronters, and challenge another only through a humble recognition of our own sin.

TYPES OF CONFRONTATION

Confrontation needs to be distinguished from interpretation: the method classically used in psychotherapy by Sigmund Freud and most of his followers. Interpretation assumes that insight, based on historical reconstruction of events in counselees' lives, is necessary for change. After hours of listening and reflecting on counselees' words, the analyst offers a so-called objective response which explains the reasons, according to analytic theory, why counselees feel the way they do and act in the manner that they have. Interpretation says little about the helper, but says something only about the one who is being helped. Like interpretation, confrontation also offers response to counselees but, unlike interpretation, it is more subjective, revealing to counselees how they appear in the counseling relationship.

The purpose of confrontation in brief pastoral counseling is to encourage counselees to consider different perspectives. Counselees are invited to explore the beliefs, attitudes, and behaviors that are harmful to themselves or others and that do not exhibit love for self, neighbor, or God. They are invited to see the gifts they possess that they ignore. They are invited to explore how Scripture or tradition speaks to their situation.

The goal for counselees is to better understand the issues they bring to counseling. Confrontation presents a different perspective and helps counselees look at issues they would not otherwise consider, at least not in the brief time that makes up most pastoral counseling contacts.

Berenson and Mitchell (1974) provide some of the most helpful material on the use of confrontation in counseling, and expand the stereotypical understanding of confrontation portrayed at the beginning of this chapter. Confrontation is more than solely pointing out individuals' weaknesses. Berenson and Mitchell distinguish between five types of confrontation. Their research, which compares the effectiveness of counselors' use of confrontation, is explored below.

Experiential Confrontation

Experiential confrontation is a way for pastors to respond to the discrepancy between their perceptions of experiences with counselees and counselees' perceptions of themselves. Such discrepancies are formed through observing the parishioner in the counseling relationship, recognizing parishioners' overt statements versus their inner experience of themselves, or recording subjective perceptions of either pastor or counselee. In experiential confrontation, the pastor verbalizes those incongruities. For example: "You said that everything has been fine in your life, but it seems to me that you are carrying the weight of the world on your shoulders."

Experiential confrontations focus on the counseling relationship. Their purpose is to help parishioners recognize that discrepancies in the counseling relationship reflect similar perceptual gaps in other relationships, whether with family members, work colleagues, or God. According to Berenson and Mitchell's research, more effective counselors use a significantly higher number of experiential confrontations than less effective counselors. More effective helpers also offer an increasing number of experiential confrontations as the counseling progresses.

Didactic Confrontation

Didactic confrontations involve teaching and informing and provide counselees with basic knowledge of things such as parenting skills, marital communication skills, and the like. In counseling, their major purpose is to provide information about the world, theology, or the helping relationship itself and to correct misinformation, thereby helping counselees to make more informed decisions. To the retired engineer who was confused about why he was not his old self six weeks after his wife's death, I suggested: "Charles, you have lost someone very dear to you. Grief is not something that is over right after the funeral. It is a slow process that can take years."

Didactic confrontations lack the dynamic intensity of experiential confrontations, and generally are less risky for the confronter. They are best used early in the counseling relationship to help counselees understand what is involved in the process. Berenson and Mitchell's research found that less effective helpers tend to let their counselees squirm uncomfortably by not giving them information about what goes on and what is expected of them in counseling. More effective helpers tell counselees what they need to know so they can best use the entire counseling process.

In brief pastoral counseling, didactic confrontations help counselees clarify theological issues, reflect on their own experience, and tie their experience to the theological themes they hear in church. For example, reconciliation with an estranged parent is tied to the reconciliation with God that we experience through Christ.

The most effective ministers use more didactic confrontations, especially those that tie theology to experience and address ethical issues in individual behavior. Unlike experiential confrontation, didactic confrontations are most beneficial at the beginning of counseling, and their usefulness diminishes over time. The reason may be that as counselees see reality more accurately on their own they need less information from the helper.

Strength and Weakness Confrontations

The third and fourth types of confrontation are *strength* and *weakness confrontations*. Strength confrontations are experiential confrontations that help counselees see their own personal resources, pointing to unused strengths they have but may have not recognized. Weakness confrontations (what most people think of when they think of confrontation) help counselees see their own liabilities. They point to what is undone, and to the pathology that exists in the self or in relationships.

A helper offering a strength confrontation might comment, "The way you resolved the conflict with the phone company suggests to me that you may have more abilities in handling conflict than you sometimes give yourself credit." A weakness confrontation addressed to a husband might be, "You are indeed honest with your wife. However, it seems to me that at times the things you say to her are not said to open up conversation or resolve your mutual problems, but to put her down so she has trouble fighting back."

In Berenson and Mitchell's research, more effective counselors use twice as many strength confrontations as do less effective ones. Conversely, less effective counselors use fifteen times as many weakness confrontations as do high level carers. Counselors' work, when evaluated by outside raters, counselees, and themselves, disclose that less effective counselors specialize in weakness confrontations. Berenson and Mitchell suggest that strength confrontations are one of the most beneficial forms of confrontation, yet one of the least used.

Neither strength nor weakness confrontations are apropos at the beginning of counseling; they become more potent as counseling progresses, as counselees begin to dig deeper within themselves and recognize things they have not looked at before. To quote Berenson and Mitchell (1974, 79–80):

> Our impression is that *strength* confrontations might have been used more often, but that their early use presents two dangers. First, most helpees are somewhat cautious at the beginning of helping and the helper probably would be seen as a 'con' if he used too many *strength* confrontations. . . . Second, the orientation of the early interviews should be toward understanding the helpee as he sees himself. Too many *strength* confrontations probably would be disruptive under such circumstances whether they were accurate or not. For these reasons, we would expect the number of *strength* confrontations to increase over time in effective helping because they would become more acceptable to the helpee.

Feminist theologians, in their valid critique of Reinhold Niebuhr and others who hold that the essence of sin is *hubris*, have contended that such a supposition has a male orientation, and for many women sin comes not from pride or a grasping for power, but from not recognizing or using their own gifts. Strength confrontations can help many people acknowledge and use their strengths and may especially help those women in counseling whose strengths society has undervalued or even shunned.

Counselors and ministers frequently have been taught that strength confrontations are unsophisticated "Pollyanna" approaches to care and that good helpers look for pathology beneath stated problems, but in brief pastoral counseling it appears that strength confrontations are some of the most useful interventions. Confrontation at its best is a way to show people their strengths, particularly those inner resources they may have overlooked. "Here," says Underwood (1985, 96), "pastors challenge people's potential."

Helpers must be truthful with counselees: they need not invent strengths. My impression, though, is that most helpers err more in failing to point out counselees' underused assets. Strength confrontation instills hope for the future and fosters a realistic view of one's abilities. Brief pastoral counseling, which by nature does not focus on pathology or take the time to break down defenses, will find strength confrontation a useful tool because it helps individuals to build upon their untapped strengths.

Encouragement to Action Confrontation

Encouragement to action confrontations are those which urge people to *do* something, to act upon their own world in some reasonable, appropriate, and ethical manner. They discourage a passive stance toward life and press people to be more proactive. After a husband has practiced behavioral rehearsal (for example, telling his feelings about the marriage to his wife), the pastor might respond: "You are doing an excellent job of expressing your feelings about your marriage here in the session. I think the next step would be for you to say at home what you have said here. Are you ready to do it? [Pause] How can you structure those conversations so that you will be comfortable in doing them?" Berenson and Mitchell (1974, 83) comment:

> The use of strength and action confrontations may demand greater sensitivity to the helpee's "phenomenological world" than the use of other confrontation categories since they very well may lead more directly to changes in healthy behavior outside the helping hour. Thus, the confronting helper must be acutely aware of how life is lived, and must be responsible for (his or her own) actions.

In their research the incidence of action confrontation, like strength confrontation, is small. Effective pastors are more adept at using encouragement to action confrontations than are less effective ones. A common deficiency in the practice of many helpers, whether psychologists, social workers, or ministers, is that they help people understand their life situation and its attendant problems but do not urge them to make specific changes. When time is brief, counselees need to sign on for the change—own it, buy into it, that is, take action. Encouragement-to-action confrontations are one way brief pastoral counseling can guide people from insight to action.

TIMING

Timing is important to all types of confrontation. The following guide offers some suggestions concerning timing.

■ Didactic confrontations are better used early on to help counselees understand the counseling process and should be used with decreasing frequency in succeeding visits.

■ Experiential confrontations are useful in the beginning and middle of counseling after the relationship has been established. Their value decreases as the process moves toward termination.

■ Strength and weakness confrontations generally are not useful at the beginning of counseling, but are more beneficial during the middle.

■ Action confrontations are most appropriate in the middle and toward the end of the counseling process when people are being urged to take steps toward change.

If pastors use any form of confrontation (other than didactic) too early in the relationship, counselees are not likely to hear them. All helpers must earn the right to be taken seriously; only as the counseling relationship develops will strength confrontations, for example, likely be believed. Theological didactic confrontations are best used after rapport has been developed by suspending judgment; then a word of grace or an ethical moment can occur.

INDIRECT CONFRONTATION

Some counselors have adopted confrontation as a lifestyle. Speaking with these persons colleague-to-colleague is like going to battle. Many of these individuals were influenced by Fritz Perls (and his Gestalt therapy) who often stated: "My job is not to comfort, but to frustrate." When ministers only comfort, they may inadvertently support people's inactivity. Confrontation, however, does not have to be direct. The ultimate goal of counseling is to get counselees to confront themselves and face their own issues rather than relying upon professionals.

When I started teaching ministers various counseling techniques, confrontation was not always well received. Some feared it would be unsupportive, while others found direct confrontation personally uncomfortable. As I reviewed my own and my supervisees' counseling practices, I recognized the liabilities of some styles of confrontation and how confrontation has been abused. For people who have had painful confrontations in the past, direct confrontation is unhelpful and more indirect methods will be needed.

When I say "indirect methods" I am not suggesting that ministers couch the confrontation in words that counselees are unable to understand. In an effort to soften the blow, helpers may actually confuse counselees. Ministers need to be honest and clear about what they are saying, but they can say it tentatively and gently. The following suggestions, if used in confrontations, may provide sufficient gentleness so that everyone feels more comfortable, and counselees do not end up fighting the helper.

■ Most important in easing the confrontation is to use all five types of confrontation, not just weakness confrontation. Perhaps nothing will help more in the acceptance of confrontation than this because weakness confrontation engenders the most resistance.

■ When beginning to confront individuals, be gentle and tentative. Ease into it. Say to a husband who is having problems with his wife, "I am wondering if you are a little irritated with your wife." The husband who is experiencing the emotion strongly might answer, "Irritated? I'm furious!" The more gentle statement better allows him to claim his emotion. Note that saying, "I'm wondering if you might feel. . ." works better than saying, "You are . . ." Most people are more likely to receive the message if it is phrased tentatively or as a question. First-person statements describe your own sense of the counselees rather than telling them what they are feeling and experiencing. An element of freedom is implied.

■ Make your confrontations as socially acceptable as possible. Most counselees have difficulty accepting something about themselves if it carries some sense of social shame. One way to defuse the stigma is to share your own experience (if it applies): "Maybe you feel the same way I often do . . ." In this case, counselees are not alone in dealing with a particular issue. When I say to counselees that they may be, say, "struggling with depression as I have struggled with it," they know that I have been there. If I need to, I can tell my story.

■ Avoid anger when you are confronting someone. Your own negative emotions can cloud the picture and the needed help may not be received. One of the more common mistakes ministers make in their pastoral counseling is that they are supportive and long-suffering until they have had all they can take, and then they give the counselee a piece of their mind. At times this cannot be avoided, but it is best to confront issues in the pastor-parishioner relationship before the minister's thinking becomes muddled by irritation or frustration, in which case there is a tendency to try to get counselees to do what you want rather than what is really most worthwhile for them.

■ If people deny what is said in a confrontation, then it is usually better to back away from the issue for the moment. If you suggest to a father who has white knuckles and pulsating temples and is pointing his finger at his daughter that he might be irritated, be prepared for him to deny any anger. Apologize and suggest that you were probably wrong. Do not forget what you said to him. Of course you may be wrong, but more likely you are correct in your assessment, and the individual was not ready to hear it. Wait until your relationship has deepened and the issue arises again. Try another confrontation, making it more tentative, socially acceptable, and gentle. If he denies it again, put it aside and wait some more. If the father continues to deny any anger, do not assume that he has not heard you. Your words may fester for days, weeks, even years.

■ A suggestion for indirect confrontation was hinted at above: share your personal experiences. Disclose things about your life that allow counselees to recognize the similar experiences in their own lives. Although not necessarily confrontive, self-disclosure presents another perspective that may challenge counselees to see a different way out of their difficulty, to see that they have the freedom to act responsibly in response to their situation.

■ A variation of self-disclosure runs as follows: "I remember in a former congregation a woman whose husband left her. It was a situation much like yours. She went through a great deal of pain. (Pause) She did a number of things that seemed to help her cope with her husband's leaving." NOTE: Whether disclosing something personal or about an unnamed parishioner from another place, such disclosures carry risks. If talking about your own experiences, determine whether counselees are able to handle what you say. Keep in mind that confidentiality is your commitment, not necessarily the counselee's. Your disclosure about, say, an affair you had many years ago or former alcohol usage may be useful in the counseling, but is likely to circulate quickly throughout the congregation. Equally important, disclosing the experiences of a former counselee—even in the past at a distant parish—may threaten confidentiality. I always disguise the cases I present (as in this book) and let counselees know they are disguised. Even so, I do such sharing only when I believe a counseling relationship is such that they will trust its confidentiality.

Some persons may be unusually open in sharing their struggles with a divorce or the loss of a child and may offer permission to relate their story to those who are going through a similar experience. (They may even offer to talk personally with someone going through the same experience.) The advantage of such disclosures is that they allow counselees to recognize that others have gone through similar experiences. They open up the helping process to a wider community, and are a very powerful way in which encouragement to action confrontations can occur.

Empathy is the essential basis of all pastoral counseling. To shorten the time needed for dealing with people's problems, however, ministers need to go beyond empathy. Confrontation stimulates growth in counselees by challenging them to take seriously issues that they have not addressed. Admittedly confrontation is not for everyone—either minister or parishioner. It can be misused; yet in the hands of a skillful minister offering brief pastoral counseling, it is an impressive tool for hastening the counseling process.

10

Depression

·ဢ

Cognitive Restructuring

Depression is the common cold of mental and emotional disorders. During any given year, according to a recent study for the National Institute of Mental Health, 15 percent of all people in the United States between the ages of eighteen and seventy-four will have significant depressive disturbances. Indeed, of all those hospitalized in a psychiatric hospital, 75 percent will report depression as part of the total cause of their treatment. Because it strikes especially during adult years when vocations are important and children are being reared, depression not only affects the individual but also has a major impact on the marriage, the family, the church, and even society.

Depression can also be a spiritual disorder. The "dark night of the soul" described by Christian mystics seems akin to, although not quite the same as, what is now termed "depression." The sense that God is absent, the doubt, and loss of meaning in religious ritual are much like many of the symptoms of depression. Even so, the seemingly similar emotions lead to different ends. For the melancholic, on the one hand, depression leads to disturbance of relations with significant others. For the Christian mystic, on the other hand, their most fundamental relationship is also changed—the relationship with God.

Further insight into depression as a spiritual problem can be gained from a study of the vice of sloth (*accidie*), one of the so-called seven deadly sins. The term *accidie* (also known as *acedia* or *akedia*) has undergone many changes of meaning through the centuries. It was first used to describe something that affected only hermit monks. By the Middle Ages *accidie* was applied to all Christians.

Accidie, at least as it was understood by the Egyptian desert monks, was a form of melancholy that affected their relationship to God. A staleness in this relationship and in religious practices frequently led the monk to avoid the ascetic observances, to feel a general

122

malaise or to sleep away time or ultimately to escape from the community and sometimes from the church.

The states described by mystics as "the dark night of the soul" or by the ascetics as *accidie* are not only the problems of a particular age or of the full-time monastic: they are common to human experience.

Throughout recorded history, one can find descriptions of depression and explanations (both psychological and environmental) for its causes. The Book of Job tells of one man's immense melancholy. In the depths of his despair Job could not imagine that his life would ever improve. He turned his anger from his parents toward God: "The terrors of God are arrayed against me" (Job 6:4). He describes his agony: "My eye has grown dim from grief, and all my members are like a shadow . . . My days are past, my plans are broken off, the desires of my heart," (Job 17:7-11).

On average, some form of depression will be felt by 15 of every 100 adults in churches during any given year. Is a depressed church member able to experience hope, or only despair? Is depression tantamount to lack of faith, and therefore sin? When the pastor speaks of faith, hope, and love, how can the individual who is depressed (who has little faith in God, others, or self, lacks hope, and feels as if no one cares) make sense out of those words? Moreover, how can a minister who is depressed speak of faith and hope? (For a more complete discussion of depression and methods of intervention other than cognitive restructuring melancholia, see Stone 1991).

DEPRESSION AND COGNITION

Depression affects people (church members and ministers among them) in every area of their lives. One area it influences is thinking. It tends to distort and misinterpret reality. Aaron Beck (1967, 255–61) offers a helpful distinction in speaking of the three major disturbed thought patterns of an individual who is depressed: viewing events, self, and the future in an idiosyncratic manner, or "the primary triad."

People who are depressed perpetually interpret events negatively, conceiving of their interactions with the world—and with God—as defeat, disparagement, abandonment, and deprivation. Neutral or even positive transactions with other people are seen as failures. Cognitively, people who are depressed evaluate their own *selves* as having less value (lower self-esteem) than when they are not depressed. They commonly indulge in blaming themselves or others and in extensive self-criticism. Guilt usually follows. Compared to others, they find themselves wanting. They also tend to be indecisive and may spend immense amounts of time trying to make a choice, often looking for the perfect solution or the right path. They view the future negatively, and feel hopelessly trapped because the future portends only continued suffering and pain. To them, time does not heal all wounds.

This cognitive set sometimes can lead to thoughts of suicide. If life seems to consist of unending and unabated suffering, and if that suffering is due to his or her own defects, then a person may view suicide as beneficial not only to self but also to friends and family.

People who are depressed experience a subtle shift in their cognitive mental organization. Certain thoughts begin to predominate to the extent that the individuals regard themselves, their experiences, and their futures negatively. Cognitive misconstructions and misperceptions follow these basic faulty information-processing efforts. Theorists on the cognitive components of depression have described six typical ways in which people who are depressed cognitively misconstrue their experience negatively (Beck 1979). These misconstructions are as follows:

Arbitrary inference. People who are depressed draw inferences counter to supportive evidence or in absence of such evidence.

Selective abstraction. People who are depressed focus on one minor detail while ignoring the more crucial features of a situation and then view the whole situation based on this one item.

Overgeneralization. As the term *overgeneralization* indicates, people who are depressed can make conclusions about themselves, their worth, and their ability to perform based on a few isolated incidents.

Magnification and minimization. Melancholic individuals do not accurately perceive events, but tend to exaggerate small, negative occurrences and render almost insignificant their positive accomplishments.

Personalization. People who are depressed may take responsibility for (usually bad) external events when little or no basis exists for such a connection.

Either/or thinking. The absolutistic, dichotomous thinking of people who are depressed categorizes all that they do in one of two opposite positions: perfect or defective, all or none, immaculate or filthy, and so on. Because they can never fit the "good" (perfect) category, they see themselves as "bad" (defective).

Most individuals who are depressed are not negative about everything. They tend to be especially sensitive to certain categories of stimuli, or triggers, that set the negative thinking in motion. Albert Ellis, one of the leaders in cognitive therapy, calls these unrealistic expectations "irrational beliefs" (Ellis and Harper 1975). According to the Ellis school of rational-emotive therapy, the emotional reaction comes last. What comes first is an activating event or experience. Next comes the person's appraisal or interpretation of the activating event, ordinarily based on one's personal beliefs (including one's implicit theology). This leads finally to the emotional reaction or consequence. If, for example, a person is angry after being rebuffed by a snooty waiter, then the rebuff itself is not the cause of the anger; the real cause is the person's thoughts about the rebuff.

In our culture's process of maturation and socialization, many people develop sets of beliefs that misconstrue experience and are counter to supporting evidence. Such are cognitive distortions because they are not supported by the reality of the cultural environment, but function nonetheless with the power of religious convictions. Ellis suggests eleven irrational beliefs or ideas most common in our society (Hauck 1972, 31–45), which follow.

1. Each adult human being absolutely must be loved or approved by virtually every significant other person in his or her community.
2. One should be thoroughly competent, adequate, and achieving in all possible respects if one is to consider oneself worthwhile.
3. Certain people are bad, wicked, or villainous and should be severely blamed and punished for their villainy.
4. It is awful—even catastrophic—when things are not the way one would like them to be.
5. Human unhappiness is externally caused, and people have little or no ability to control their sorrows and disturbances.

6. If something is or may be dangerous or fearsome, then one should be terribly concerned about it and should keep dwelling on the possibility of its occurring.

7. Certain difficulties and responsibilities in life are easier to avoid than to face.

8. One should be dependent upon others; one needs someone stronger than oneself upon whom to rely.

9. One's history is an all-important determinant of one's present behavior, and because something once strongly affected one's life, it should now definitely have a similar effect.

10. One should become very upset over other people's problems and disturbances.

11. Human problems have one invariable right and perfect solution, and catastrophe will likely befall should this perfect solution not be found.

Academic theologians are correct in criticizing the care and counseling offered by pastors who do not concern themselves with the troubled person's theology or beliefs. Many upsetting emotional reactions and problem behaviors seen by the pastor arise because of an individual's *implicit* theology. Many counselors could relate cases in which distortions of the Christian faith (a misunderstanding of the idea of sin or a fear of punishment by an angry God for some minor infraction, for example) have caused problems in people's lives. Individuals' responses to many situations are determined by the way they understand the events, not by the events themselves.

COUNSELING PEOPLE WHO ARE DEPRESSED

Cognitive theorists believe that an unadaptive or upsetting emotional response (depression being one of several) arises from a person's indiscriminate and automatic labeling of a situation. The extent to which a situation is labeled or identified according to irrational ideas, such as those listed by Ellis, determines how extreme an unwanted emotion or action will be.

We do not purposely tell ourselves such cognitive misconstructions in real-life situations. What plagues us, rather, is the automatic generation of these detrimental beliefs. Much *automatic labeling* occurs instantaneously and, after years of habitual response, is outside of our awareness.

When a person who claims to be depressed or who has many of the symptoms of depression comes for help, the minister needs from the beginning to discern whether the person is in fact depressed or has some other configuration of emotions or possibly a physical illness. Because both the experience of depression and its precipitators vary considerably from one individual to another, the minister must learn the specific ways in which the counselee is experiencing the dysphoria (feelings of being unwell or unhappy) and what might be causing or exacerbating it.

During this same time, determining the extent and severity of the depression is critical. Degrees to which melancholic people are depressed vary considerably. The episodic and transitory "blues" that most experience, lasting a few hours or a few days, is not depression. Uncomfortable as those moments are, they are not of significant scope or duration.

Some depression is so severe that medication and/or hospitalization are needed. The majority of individuals whom pastors encounter, however, are only mildly depressed and can be offered skillful and much needed brief pastoral counseling. One intervention for handling depression and similar negative emotions is called cognitive restructuring. Such pastoral care is not second-class treatment, but is exactly the quality of care that is required with such cases.

COGNITIVE RESTRUCTURING

Interventions have been designed to change individuals' learned negative cognitions and to teach them a new set of beliefs more based in reality. How does one change another's cognitions? Not easily! Ministers who are trained in pastoral care and counseling and who also have a background in theology and philosophy probably are the best equipped of all helping professionals to enable people to change their beliefs. The church generally has acknowledged (although post–1950s pastoral counseling practice sometimes has not) that our beliefs about the future, self, others, the world, and God greatly affect how we act. (Cognitive psychological theorists recognize this as well, but state it in nontheological terms.) Cognitive restructuring is helping people to see the world more realistically and to change unfounded beliefs, misconceptions, and expectations. As a practical intervention, it can be used in brief pastoral counseling and includes the following steps:

Assessment. The first task of the minister (and of counselees) is to try to understand the core negative assumptions or misconceived

127

beliefs that people who are depressed hold about themselves, God, and the world.

Teaching–Learning. The next task is to help people who are depressed change their erroneous beliefs. Exposing cognitive misconceptions is the easy part of the process; relearning is much more difficult. It can be facilitated by explaining how people develop faulty information processing mechanisms or irrational beliefs.

Practicing. The third step moves from educating people who are depressed about their negative misconceptions to the actual practice of catching themselves: Counselees recognize their own irrational thoughts and reformulate them in ways more based in reality. They may not recognize their cognitive misconceptions immediately, and sometimes not for several days. When they are suddenly overcome with a wave of depression, they are urged to stop and mentally back up to find the trigger of the depression and identify their automatic unrealistic thoughts and beliefs.

Of the various schools of cognitive therapy, several of the more readily accessible authors associated with them are Beck (1979, 1989), David Burns (1980), Ellis and Harper (1975), and Paul Hauck (1972, 1980). Although ideas will be drawn from all of these authors, the method of cognitive restructuring presented here will rely more heavily upon Rational-Emotive Therapy (RET). Such reliance, however, should not be construed as endorsing RET over the others.

Karen Peterson was making a pastoral call in the hospital, visiting a member of her congregation who had undergone minor surgery. Her parishioner requested, "Please stop for a few minutes and see the man next to me. He is very despondent and tried to end his life." Pastor Peterson acted promptly on the suggestion. She spent only a few minutes with Allen Waldon, but to her surprise he phoned her some months later and said he had to see her.

Upon entering Pastor Peterson's office, Allen, a twenty-nine-year-old draftsman, told her that his wife had left him to marry another man. He felt totally lost without her and had attempted suicide. "I wouldn't do that again, though. I feel horrible about her leaving," he said, "but I don't want to go through *that* again."

Allen was shy and had dated only one woman other than his wife. He was a perfectionist and demanded so much of himself that he believed no one—especially a woman—would ever want to talk to him, let alone spend an evening with him. He could not imagine anyone wanting to be with him because he felt he was so uninteresting.

Assessment

The first task Allen and the pastor faced was that of assessment. Together they had to determine which cognitive misperceptions and distortions were troubling him. Pastor Peterson, after explaining how irrational thoughts can cause painful feelings and actions, asked Allen to read Paul Hauck's *Overcoming Depression*.

Brief pastoral counseling attempts to involve counselees in the assessment task and uses homework assignments. Homework is especially useful for cognitive restructuring because it helps counselees determine for themselves what irrational ideas or cognitive misperceptions they make. For homework, they read a book or portion of a book between sessions. The pastor might hand the book to the counselee and say something like, "*You* diagnose *yourself*. Read this, assess yourself, and determine which irrational ideas are plaguing you. It may not be easy to admit some of your irrational beliefs. In fact, it can be downright embarrassing. But the more honest you allow yourself to be, the quicker you can bring some relief to your problems.

In Allen's case, he returned the next week and, referring to Ellis's list of eleven irrational ideas (see above), said, "I've got one, two, four, five, and seven." After some conversation, Pastor Peterson suggested that Allen may also be troubled by number eight. He admitted the possibility: "I thought of it, but it's hard for a man to admit he might be dependent. I thought maybe it was because I was shy."

Teaching–Learning

After the initial assessment process, the task is to help counselees change their beliefs or cognitive information processing errors. This is the heart of cognitive restructuring. For some people, this is a simple process requiring only a session or two, while for others it is an arduous task, requiring more time. In Allen's case, his pain was great, and he was quite willing to face his irrational beliefs squarely.

There are many methods of cognitive restructuring available. In some situations one method may suffice. In others, the pastoral

129

counselor's creativity may be stretched to match resources with needs. A rational-emotive therapist like Ellis might confront and challenge directly the counselees' irrational beliefs until they come to a more realistic view of the world. Such a rational-emotive therapy session can be explosive, with counselor and counselee at times coming to verbal blows. This kind of confrontation needs to be used with considerable sensitivity (see chap. 9 on confrontation). Once a good rapport has been established, increasing confrontation and challenging can be used. This type of cognitive restructuring is not for everyone and therefore will not be useful for all pastors. It is not my first choice.

Allen's self-confidence did not seem high enough for such a head-on approach. Pastor Peterson thought that a better way to begin cognitive restructuring with Allen was first to explain the theory behind the process—how a person's beliefs determine his or her emotions—and then to review Ellis's eleven irrational beliefs (or Burns's ten cognitive distortions; 1980).

Using numerous examples to identify inaccurate assumptions or beliefs is beneficial. Illustrations may be drawn from some of the books listed in the bibliography or, even better, from personal experiences from the minister's or counselee's life. Karen Peterson hit upon an effective example in her work with Allen. She said: "Think of two students taking an art class on sketching the human figure. While they are both working at their easels, the teacher circulates around the room, offering criticism to help the students improve at a very difficult skill—drawing the human body. One student thinks to herself that she is glad this teacher offers plenty of criticism so that each student can become a better artist. She also believes that the teacher's criticism shows interest in her work. The other student starts to worry when the instructor comes near him. He thinks the teacher is too critical and should tell students only positive things to encourage them. Now, because the professor is giving criticism equally to all the students, what is the difference between the two?"

Pastor Peterson's approach involved a teaching process. Teaching can be helpful because it often enables counselees to see that irrational thoughts cause emotional turmoil. One counselor I know uses visual aids, although in a somewhat risky manner. In counseling, he will turn around in his chair, take a rubber snake from his desk drawer, and throw it on the floor near the counselee. The counselee may jump or even scream. The counselor then shows the person

130

that the snake is made of rubber. He explains that how we feel about an object is greatly dependent on how we think about it—that is, whether we identify it as a rubber snake or a real one. This method is not recommended, but it illustrates well the kind of creativity that a pastor can use in explaining these principles.

In the learning process, the pastor needs to demonstrate rational thinking and the process of rational reevaluation. This can be done in all sectors of ministry but especially in the counseling office. Pastor Peterson, for example, shared with Allen some effective and ineffective ways in which she had handled difficult situations and how her beliefs affected them. She believed wholeheartedly in what she was trying to help Allen achieve (changing his irrational beliefs). If she did not, she would have been far less effective.

Practicing

The focus of cognitive restructuring soon needs to shift from teaching about the process to practicing it. Allen was told that he would now need to both identify his own irrational thoughts and then rethink them. Pastor Peterson urged Allen to practice and do homework.

I tell counselees that whenever they catch themselves getting upset or depressed or acting in problematic ways, they should stop at once and identify the cue or trigger that set off that behavior. They are to ask themselves: What irrational idea is at the root of my problem? What unspoken assumption is causing this upset? What am I uncritically telling myself? The thrust of Pastor Peterson's counseling with Allen was the following:

PASTOR: Think back to what you told me about last Friday, when you wanted to ask one of your fellow employees at the office for a date after work and you became upset that you never asked her. You remember that?

ALLEN: Do I ever! If that keeps happening I'll never ever go out with anyone.

PASTOR: OK. Try to remember and ask yourself, "What was I telling myself that caused me to be so upset?"

131

ALLEN: [Pause] Well, I was embarrassed.

PASTOR: Uh-huh. I'll bet you were. But what things were you telling yourself?

ALLEN: I don't know. [Pause] I don't remember.

PASTOR: I know you were saying certain things to yourself—probably not "She hates me, so I can't do it," but something like that. What do you imagine you were saying to yourself that stopped you from asking her and created your anxiety?

ALLEN: [Pause] I suppose I thought she would say no. [Pause]

PASTOR: Yes! You thought she would say no, and that would be . . .

ALLEN: And that would be awful.

PASTOR: Would it?

ALLEN: Yes. . . . Well, no [pause] . . . When you really think about it. I wouldn't like it, but it wouldn't be *awful*. [Pause] But it's just that I haven't done anything like that since I was in high school.

PASTOR: I think you're beginning to get the idea. Again, I'd like you to ask yourself, "What other irrational things am I telling myself that keep me from approaching her? How am I hindering myself in asking her out?"

It takes time to help counselees discover the problematic things they are telling themselves, like Allen's "It would be awful." Notice that Karen Peterson responded positively to Allen's groping observations—she praised his every attempt at identifying an irrational statement. Positive reinforcement is important. If people sense that they are making progress, as the pastor's praise suggests, then their situations will not seem nearly so hopeless. Thus counselees are taught to regard any upset or aberrant behavior as a cue that they may be operating out of unrealistic beliefs or expectations, and they need to stop in their tracks, ferret out the irrational things they have been telling themselves (their cognitive misperceptions), and replace them with thinking that is squarely based in reality.

Sometimes, however, the minister can play the devil's advocate or reverse roles. At one point when Allen seemed quite resistant to change, Karen Peterson said, "Let's try something different." Rising to her feet, she went on: "Let's change chairs. You be the pastor, and I'll be you." Before Allen even had a chance to consider, much less complain, she was verbalizing what she believed to be the irrational things he was thinking, and suddenly it was Allen's task, acting now as pastor/counselor, to refute them. When I use this technique, I frequently exaggerate. I formulate the irrational statements as sharply as possible so that counselees can see their position as clearly as possible. For some, this kind of reversal can bring great insight.

Counselees do not usually catch cues well at first, and Allen was no exception. Two days after the session, he belatedly had an "aha!" experience, suddenly recognizing the reason he had been upset and what the originating cues actually were. I usually tell counselees that they may not identify these cues immediately, that it may take several days at first, then perhaps several hours, and that only after considerable practice will they begin to catch cues right on the spot. Eventually, though, with enough experience in catching cues and replacing distorted thoughts and faulty information-processing efforts with ones based in reality, the problem will diminish or even disappear. Cognitive restructuring involves give-and-take in conversation aimed at helping counselees find the ways they cognitively distort reality and then replacing their irrational beliefs with accurate perceptions.

ADDITIONAL COGNITIVE RESTRUCTURING METHODS

Other methods of brief pastoral counseling are useful for helping counselees change their thinking: thought stopping, worry time, blowup technique, alternative technique, reattribution, behavioral rehearsal, imaging, bibliotherapy, and spiritual direction. What follows is a brief description of a few of the more useful methods (see also Stone 1988, 1991).

133

The Alternative Technique

A technique called "the alternative technique" is especially useful for people who systematically and negatively bias all their interpretations of stimuli and events. The pastor explains to the counselees some of the more common cognitive information-processing distortions people make, and together they discuss specific experiences in the counselees' lives. They then construct explanations for events that are different from the earlier, distorted interpretations. The task for depressed individuals is to recognize their negative biases and substitute more accurate interpretations of their experiences. This technique serves as a basis for problem management; counselees consider and strategize alternative ways of handling problems based on a new interpretation of the circumstances.

Reattribution

Reattribution, a cognitive intervention somewhat similar to the alternative technique, helps depressed counselees to correctly assign responsibility or blame for negative events that happen to them. Working together with the pastor, they apply the laws of logic and common sense as well as a sound understanding of ethics to a variety of negative incidents in their lives, trying to determine realistic responsibility for their occurrence. The goal is not to absolve individuals of responsibility, but to note the many factors that can contribute to any bad situation.

Reattribution serves to lift the weight of self-reproach, search for ways of salvaging troublesome situations, and prevent recurrences. It can help people to accept responsibility for *real* guilt and *real* sin, but not take blame for imagined sins. Reattribution of major negative events (such as divorce) can be followed by the traditional pastoral methods of confession, forgiveness, absolution, and amendment of life. The pastor should be alert, however, to a dangerous pattern that Roy Fairchild (1980, 33) suggests many Christians pursue: "[Depressed persons] move from guilty feelings to atonement to attempted redemption by placating and obeying, by overworking, by denying themselves pleasure, and by subtle self-sabotage or clear self-destruction."

The recent tendency of the church to minimize or even ignore sin (Capps 1993), except as part of some global social issue, is an immense loss for depressives. Most feel they are truly sinful and have done wrong (and indeed they *are* sinful and *have* done wrong). The minister who little believes in sin or offers grace too glibly does not take seriously people who are depressed or their experience and leaves them to grapple with their gnawing guilt alone, unaided by their spiritual guide.

Behavioral Rehearsal

In behavioral rehearsal (see chap. 7), the counselee simply runs through the frightening scenario, simulating it in the counseling session before encountering it in real life. Allen Waldon's minister could have had him practice asking the coworker out for an evening meal. Pastor Peterson would set up the behavioral rehearsal by first reviewing the scene with Allen, then suggesting that while the scene is being re-created, he say out loud any distorted thoughts that occur, immediately replacing them with ones based in reality. The pastor could also tell Allen that she will at times function as his alter ego, saying out loud some of the things he may be thinking but not verbalizing. He is to incorporate her words into his own thinking, refuting any of the irrational statements she makes. In re-creating the situation, Pastor Peterson also could play the part of the coworker or have Allen play both parts.

In behavioral rehearsal for cognitive restructuring, the words exchanged are less important than the thinking process of the counselee because the goal is to change any cognitive misconstructions or unfounded beliefs. The advantage of behavioral rehearsal for brief pastoral counseling is that it highlights counselees' cognitive distortions as they occur in the counseling session. Therefore, the conversation is not about a past event, but the present.

One important caution about behavioral rehearsal: Counselees should not prematurely take on situations that are too threatening. If this seems possible, then the pastor needs to slow things down by developing a graded list of less stressful situations that can be practiced first, before tackling the troublesome event. In Allen's case, because he already knew his coworker well, an easier or less threatening rehearsal would be just to stop by her desk and say hello. This could be practiced a few times before rehearsing the scenario of asking her out for a date. If even this is too troubling, then a still less threatening scene for behavioral rehearsal might be merely to *think* about saying hello to her the next day.

Imaging

Imaging as a brief counseling intervention is often more beneficial than behavioral rehearsal for depressed people. It is much like a guided daydream (see chap. 6). For example, instead of actually asking the secretary for a date, or even practicing rehearsing it, Allen would simply *imagine* doing it, closing his eyes and visualizing the event as if it were occurring. The major difference between daydreaming and imaging, of course, has to do with articulation. In imaging, counselees are instructed to say aloud all of the events that happen, as well as to express verbally the attendant feelings and the thoughts that occur to them.

Counselees image themselves going through all of the steps involved in a certain activity and then discuss specific roadblocks and potential conflicts that might arise while actually doing the activity. They report all irrational thoughts that occur and attempt to correct them. They are urged to pay special attention to every detail and then to work out strategies for carrying out the activity in real life. They imagine the activity additional times to discover any other cognitive misconceptions and to begin feeling comfortable with the step-by-step process required for carrying out the act. The minister needs to be aware that individuals who are quite depressed may have difficulty concentrating, as their minds may wander. If this is the case, patience and gentle urging are required.

Bibliotherapy

A final brief pastoral counseling intervention for changing cognition is bibliotherapy, or reading. Books such as Paul Hauck's *Overcoming Depression* (1973), *Overcoming Worry and Fear* (1975), and *Overcoming Frustration and Anger* (1974); Albert Ellis's *A New Guide to Rational Living* (1975); David Burns' *Feeling Good* (1980); and Aaron Beck's *Love Is Never Enough* (1989) are valuable resources that should be read particularly by persons who can identify with the problems addressed in the books.

Allen, like most counselees, found a couple of situations in *Overcoming Depression* that were similar to his own. He was a quick learner and, like many people, once he started having some success in catching his cognitive distortions and finding emotional relief, made a decided break with his former ways of thinking. Allen's new way of thinking and acting was self-reinforcing. When he finally got up enough nerve to ask his colleague out, sure enough, she turned him down. Allen was nonplussed by her refusal, but using the principles he had already learned he handled it so well emotionally that it gave him further confidence to deal with new situations and eventually to have some success in relating to other women.

Depression usually does not wriggle and squirm, act out and disrupt class, or rob banks. It is more likely to sit quietly in the corner, not wanting to be a bother. In its quietness, it frequently is not noticed until its silence becomes so powerful that problems like job performance deterioration, reclusiveness, marital difficulties, and even suicide, become obvious.

Cognitive restructuring methods are well suited to brief pastoral counseling for a wide range of problems, among them depression, and their effectiveness can be long-lived. Cognitive restructuring is particularly appropriate to the counseling offered by pastors, whose theological perspective and communal context underscore their interest in and attention to the fundamental matters of thought, attitude, and belief.

11

Anxiety and Tension
~
Relaxation Training

Modern life is filled with dangers. The urban jungle, the suburbs, and increasingly even rural areas present us with situations in which we experience threat and attack. Our responses to such situations throw us back to our origins. Much like Paleolithic cave dwellers stalked or attacked by wild animals, our whole system reacts immediately. Adrenaline pumps into our blood, which flows to the control areas of our body, giving us the strength to act. Heartbeat accelerates, muscles tense, the body readies itself either to tangle with the threat or flee quickly.

What is so marvelous about human bodies, then or now, is that this fight-or-flight response, this instant reaction to danger, occurs whether the peril is a wild animal, a car swerving into our path in rush hour traffic, or a letter from the IRS auditors. But an important difference exists between how humans handled these fight-or-flight situations in the primeval forests of the Stone Age and how we handle them now. Then, humans actually fought or fled, thus using up the adrenaline in their blood. Now, our hearts may pound for a while after the threat has passed, the veins in our foreheads may throb, but we have not exercised our muscles or burned up the adrenaline.

As dangers and stresses multiply in our lives, our bodies tend to remain in a low-level state of arousal, constantly ready for action. This keyed-up state is what is often termed *anxiety* or *tension*. Instead of feeling the good exhaustion that follows vigorous exercise, we feel drained, our stomach tied in knots and head pounding. We have trouble getting to sleep at night, or we may too quickly become edgy at another's words or actions. Instead of being able to fight or flee as our distant ancestors did, we live with the anxiety-creating situations, seeking escape by swallowing Valium, drinking beer, or anesthetizing ourselves in front of the television. For many in today's hectic society, anxiety is a constant, a way of life. Some ways of handling it, however, are more appropriate than others.

A CASE OF ANXIETY

Madeline Perez was glad she was not drinking excessively like her friend, but she knew she had to do something about her nerves when her dentist declared her a "tooth grinder" and hinted that she might need to see somebody about it because "it could be emotional." It was emotional; Madeline had known for some time that something was wrong, but she had been afraid to face it. Besides, she was so busy. In fact, that was part of her problem.

Her husband Mike had decided after seven years in the Navy that he did not want to make a career of it. He returned to college, and Madeline had to go to work. It was hard for both of them, and hard for their two preschool children. Mike was studying constantly, it seemed, plus working almost full time. Madeline served as secretary for a tyrant. She detested working in an office, but said, "It's all I can do and, besides, the pay is OK." Most of all she hated sending her two daughters to nursery school. She had always thought that a mother should be at home when her children are young. She felt guilty.

Madeline was on edge all the time. She was taking medication for her frequent tension headaches, and hated using medication, but saw no way out. Perhaps she was not exactly at the end of her rope, but Madeline knew it was time to do something. Her first thought was to call Pastor Brian Stuber. Although she had been critical of him in the past for doing too much counseling and not enough of his churchly duties, she knew that he was a good counselor. One of her friends in the adult class had assured her of that.

As Madeline and Pastor Stuber reviewed her different problems, they found a number of items potentially related to anxiety:

- Grinding her teeth

- Tension headaches

- Sleeping problems

- Fatigue

- Feeling pressure from all sides

- Guilt about using child-care for her daughters

- A lack of support from her husband

Three brief pastoral counseling approaches were used in Madeline's case. First, the pastor helped her to clarify her thinking and become aware of the ways in which she was upsetting herself (cognitive interventions, discussed in chap. 10). Pastor Stuber thereby helped her address her feelings of guilt and anxiety about her daughters. He shared recent research findings showing that children in a group child-care situation often progress faster and develop more skill in learning and in interpersonal relationships than do children who are raised exclusively in their own homes.

Second, Madeline and her pastor together applied problem management methods to the situation, looking for ways in which she could simplify her life and cut some stress-producing stimuli (problem management, discussed in chap. 3). Madeline was committed to helping her husband get his degree, but Pastor Stuber also suggested that she find ways to "do something for Madeline." She decided to trade baby-sitting chores with a neighbor so that she and her husband could enjoy an occasional weekend camping in the mountains alone, and she guessed she might afford one nice restaurant lunch a week with her coworkers at the office. She made several other changes to simplify her life and to treat herself to some more relaxing times.

The immediate problem was still that Madeline suffered from too much anxiety. Pastor Stuber believed that a third approach, *relaxation training,* could be helpful, and much of their counseling time was spent in this way. Madeline had belonged to an early morning prayer group in the church before Mike left the Navy, but she dropped it when she went back to work.

In the prayer group Pastor Stuber had recently been using autogenic training (described below) with the prayer group to help them relax and to assist them in focusing their thoughts and concerns. He suggested that Madeline rejoin the group and renew her daily devotional life at a set time each morning while her husband took responsibility for the children; at this time she also was to practice her autogenic exercises.

The pastor led her through relaxation exercises during their second session together and recorded his words on a cassette tape recorder. (He made his own tapes and gave her one, but he could have used one of the prerecorded tapes that are widely available.) Madeline quickly got into the exercises and the daily devotional time at home. She noticed the change immediately in her sleeping. At her next session, she reported jubilantly: "I've had my first good night's sleep since I returned to work." It took a bit longer for her to discern any effect on her headaches, and at least four weeks went by before their frequency had greatly diminished. Even after the counseling was terminated, whenever she became tense she recognized it first in the form of a headache. One of the benefits of relaxation training is that people develop a sensitivity to their bodies, which frequently signal that something is wrong before they otherwise would notice.

RELAXATION TRAINING

How do you go about training someone to relax? Most of us have had the experience of consciously trying to calm down and only ending up more tense than before. If Pastor Stuber had advised Madeline to "just relax," then her inability to do so would have become an additional frustration and would have led to even greater tension and anxiety.

It is manifest from both a medical and a psychological point of view that for some people, learning physical relaxation is helpful in reducing emotional stress. With the addition of some cognitive procedures (such as those covered in chapter 10), these relaxation methods can be even more beneficial.

The human brain has a feedback system that includes tension sensors in the muscle cells which signal the muscles to tense for action when fear triggers the need, such as the cave dweller's chance meeting with a wild animal or the freeway driver's encounter with a car swerving into the lane. Unfortunately, in modern society muscular action is not required in most situations. When anxiety and muscle tension are prolonged, the control center in the brain becomes set, like a thermostat, to higher and higher levels of tolerable muscle tension. The increased tension of the muscles can keep the mind apprehensive, and the apprehension in turn triggers increased muscle tension. This vicious cycle can be broken by focusing either on how we think about certain anxiety-provoking situations, which can result in reduced muscle tension, or on how we can train to relax, which can relieve the troubled thinking and calm the anxiety by releasing tension in the body's muscles. Ideally, brief pastoral counseling will do both—train parishioners in relaxation methods and help them address their cognitive distortions and make different choices in their environment so as to reduce the potential for stress.

WHEN RELAXATION METHODS WORK

What types of people can be helped in brief pastoral counseling by relaxation techniques? The simple answer is that almost everyone suffers from anxiety in one form or another and can be a candidate for such a remedy. Certain situations, however, can make these methods more appropriate or productive than others.

Because anxiety and relaxation are almost always inversely related—that is, more of one usually results in less of the other—relaxation methods can be helpful in cases of various ailments involving *physical* tension. People suffering from disorders such as migraine or tension headaches, ulcers, overbreathing, gastrointestinal ailments, and lower back pain (particularly those which doctors have determined are caused by tension and are not physiologically based) can be aided with relaxation methods. Relaxation methods can also be beneficial for those who grind their teeth, suffer insomnia, and experience certain sexual dysfunctions, such as impotence in men and preorgasmic difficulties with women.

Relaxation methods also are helpful for *emotional and interpersonal* problems in which tension exists. They are useful for people with phobias, extensive anger, and job tension. I found that several family relationships were transformed when, for example, one spouse came home carrying the tension and pressure of the job, while the other spouse, cooped up all day with preschool children, was ready to get out of the home. Relaxation training prepared this couple to tolerate the frustrations of opposing needs, cope better with the day's problems, and to reenter the family relationship each evening with less bickering and greater opportunity for mutual understanding and support.

Obsessive or worrying thoughts either can cause or accompany increased anxiety. Such thoughts may focus on some feared external threat or the fear of some psychological or physiological harm. For example, an individual who is to speak at a sales meeting may fear that she will forget what she is to say. A person who will be attending a play in a crowded theatre may fear that in the middle of the performance, he will have to search for a rest room. These worries may become obsessive, triggering physiological tension that in turn triggers additional obsessive thoughts and fears. They also can lead to avoidance or escape moves by individuals. Relaxation training calms obsessive thoughts, clears impaired thinking, and helps people to be less prone to avoidance or escapist behaviors.

In contrast, people who do not benefit from relaxation training are those individuals who for physical or mental reasons are not able to practice the exercises. Individuals with multiple phobias or a protracted history of severe anxiety also may not be candidates for relaxation training. Additionally, because anxiety sometimes can mask depression, when the level of anxiety is lowered depression may come to the fore. If depression is suspected, then the minister must move with some caution before attempting to lessen the anxiety.

A few physical ailments have symptoms similar to anxiety, such as paroxysmal tachycardia, hypoglycemia, and drug withdrawal (Kennerley 1990, 14–15). Although diagnosis of such diseases is not within the minister's purview, referral to the family physician is in order whenever such a physical disorder is suspected.

When anxiety is clearly a secondary symptom of a greater difficulty, such as marital distress, relaxation training may be useful, but other methods need to be employed as the primary interventions.

RELAXATION METHODS

Individuals who are anxious can be trained in brief pastoral counseling to relax, and a number of ways are available for doing this: progressive muscle relaxation, autogenic training, biofeedback, hypnosis and self-hypnosis, yoga, Transcendental Meditation, heart-lung exercise (jogging, for example), controlled breathing, medication, and prayer. Some of these methods are only marginally helpful, but others are easily adaptable to the pastor's work. Three very effective methods of relaxation training are discussed here.

Progressive Relaxation

First developed in the 1930s by University of Chicago physician Edmund Jacobson (Jacobson 1974), progressive relaxation was not practiced extensively until the 1950s when Joseph Wolpe (1964) adapted it for his work.

The following is a transcript of a progressive relaxation method I have used for reducing muscle tension. (Words in parentheses in this and subsequent exercises are alternative phrases or instructions for the helper.) The words are those of the minister:

> Let your eyelids be lightly closed or partially open. Adopt a let-it-happen, passive attitude and let relaxation occur at its own pace. If your mind wanders to other thoughts, don't worry; gently let them pass by and calmly come back to doing the exercise.
>
> Now become aware of your body. Scan over it. Notice how it feels.
>
> Become aware of your right arm and hand. Notice how they feel. Keeping the other muscles of your body relaxed, extend your right arm straight out in front of you while pulling your hand back at the wrist. Hold it. (Hold five to seven seconds in this and the following segments.) / Sense the tension building. . . . Now relax your hand, lower your arm while imagining and feeling the tension flowing out and the relaxation flowing in. Let your arm and hand be loose and limp, heavy and relaxed. Feel the relaxation.
>
> Now shift your attention to your left arm and hand. Notice how they feel. Keeping the other muscles of your body relaxed, extend your left arm straight out in front of you while pulling your hand back at the wrist. Hold it. / Sense the tension building. . . . Now relax your hand, lower your arm while imagining and feeling the tension flowing out and the relaxation flowing in. Let your arm and hand be loose and limp, heavy and relaxed. Feel the relaxation.
>
> Now become aware of both your arms and hands. Notice how they feel. Keeping the other muscles of your body relaxed, extend both arms straight out in front of you. Now make a tight fist with both hands. Hold it. / Sense the tension building. . . . Now relax your hands, lower your arms while imagining and feeling the tension flowing out and the relaxation flowing in. Let your arms and hands be loose and limp, heavy and relaxed. Feel the relaxation.
>
> Shift your attention to your right leg and foot. Notice how they feel. Keeping the other muscles of your body relaxed, extend your right leg straight out in front of you and pull your right foot and toes back toward you. Hold it. / Sense the tension building. . . . Now relax your right foot and toes, lower your leg while imagining and feeling the tension flowing out and the relaxation flowing in. Let your right leg and foot be loose and limp, heavy and relaxed. Feel the relaxation.
>
> Become aware of your left leg and foot. Notice how they feel. Keeping the other muscles of your body relaxed, extend your left leg

straight out in front of you and pull your left foot and toes back toward you. Hold it. / Sense the tension building. . . . Now relax your left foot and toes, lower your leg while imagining and feeling the tension flowing out and the relaxation flowing in. Let your left leg and foot be loose and limp, heavy and relaxed. Feel the relaxation.

Now shift your attention to both your legs and feet. Notice how they feel. Keeping the other muscles of your body relaxed, extend both legs straight out in front of you while pressing your feet and toes forward. Hold it. / Sense the tension building. . . . Now relax your feet and toes, lower your feet and legs while imagining and feeling the tension flowing out and the relaxation flowing in. Let your legs and feet be loose and limp, heavy and relaxed. Feel the relaxation.

Now become aware of your chest and abdomen. Notice how they feel. Keeping the other muscles of your body relaxed, pull your abdomen in tightly and expand your chest. Hold it. / Sense the tension building. . . . Now relax your abdomen and chest while imagining and feeling the tension flowing out and the relaxation flowing in. Let your chest and abdomen be loose and limp, heavy and relaxed. Feel the relaxation.

Now shift your attention to your back. Notice how it feels. Keeping the other muscles of your body relaxed and your breathing calm and regular, pull your shoulders straight back while gently arching your upper back backward, allowing your abdomen and pelvis to go forward. Hold it. / Feel the tension building. . . . Now relax your back while imagining and feeling the tension flowing out and the relaxation flowing in. Let your entire back be loose and limp, heavy and relaxed. Feel the relaxation.

Now shift your attention to your shoulders, neck, and face. Notice how they feel. Keeping the other muscles of your body relaxed, raise your shoulders up toward your ears, keeping your lower arms relaxed, and gently press your head backward while clenching your jaws tightly together and squeezing your eyelids closed. Hold it but keep breathing. / Feel the tension building. . . . Now lower your shoulders, relax your neck, jaws, and eyes and your entire face, while imagining and feeling the tension flowing out and the relaxation flowing in. Let your shoulders and neck be loose and limp, heavy and relaxed, your jaw loose and slack, your eyes relaxed and calm, and your entire face soft and relaxed. Feel the relaxation in your shoulders, neck, and face.

Now scan over your entire body and sense the good feelings of relaxation that exist in your mind and body.

Now I'm going to count, slowly, from one to five. At the count of five, take a deep breath. When inhaling, mentally say, "Mind alert, wide awake," and open your eyes. On the exhale say, "Relaxed and refreshed." One. Coming up. Two. Three. Four. Five. Breathe in deeply. Say, "Mind alert, wide awake," and open your eyes. Exhale saying, "Relaxed and refreshed." Gently stretch all your muscles, then slowly get up, feeling alert and refreshed.

The effective use of progressive relaxation requires variation and individualization for each counselee, taking into consideration the special needs or physical conditions of that particular person (for example, back or neck trouble). When people become familiar with the method, the amount of detailed description of how to relax particular muscle groups can be reduced greatly. In the period of five to seven seconds during which the muscles are held tense, they should be quite tight, but never to the point of pain. At first, not all parts of the body may be covered; but as practice sharpens counselees' skill, they can add other body areas as needed.

Autogenic Exercises

A second method of relaxation that can be used in brief pastoral counseling was developed by Schultz and Luthe (1959). Autogenic training trains individuals to relax muscles not through physical exercises, as in progressive relaxation, but by mental control. As with progressive relaxation, most counselees probably will not be able to do all areas of the body during the first practice sessions. One possible transcript for autogenic relaxation follows.

> Let your eyelids be lightly closed or partially open. Adopt a let-it-happen, passive attitude and let relaxation occur at its own pace.
>
> Become aware of your body. Scan over it. Notice how it feels. Take several deep breaths and allow your whole body to relax.
>
> Now just let your breathing be natural, calm, and regular. Stay a passive observer of your environment but label whatever comes into your awareness. If it is a sound you hear, mentally say "sound." If it is a feeling, say "feeling." If it is a memory, say "memory." If it is a fantasy, say "fantasy." Just do this for a while (a minute or so). /
>
> Now imagine yourself alone, lying on a warm, sunny beach (or floating on an air mattress in a backyard pool, or taking a hot bath), or in any other warm and relaxing situation. See yourself lying there, calm, warm, and comfortable, without a care in the world. Feel the relaxation.
>
> Become aware of your right arm and hand. Each time you exhale, mentally say, "My right arm is heavy (relaxed) and warm." Imagine warmth (relaxation) flowing down your arm, into your hand, and all the way to your fingertips. Allow your breathing to be calm

and regular. Now just let your right arm and hand be loose and limp, warm and relaxed. Feel the warmth and relaxation.

Now shift your attention to your left arm and hand. Each time you exhale, mentally say, "My left arm is heavy (relaxed) and warm." Imagine warmth (relaxation) flowing down your arm, into your hand, and all the way to your fingertips. Allow your breathing to be calm and regular. Now let your left arm and hand be loose and limp, warm and relaxed. Feel the warmth and relaxation.

Now become aware of your right leg and foot. Each time you exhale, mentally say, "My right leg and foot are heavy (relaxed) and warm." Imagine warmth flowing down your leg and into your foot. Allow your breathing to be calm and regular. Now let your right leg and foot be loose and limp, warm and relaxed. Feel the warmth and relaxation.

Now shift your attention to your left leg and foot. Each time you exhale, mentally say, "My left leg and foot are heavy (relaxed) and warm." Imagine warmth flowing down your leg and into your foot. Allow your breathing to be calm and regular. Now just let your left leg and foot be loose and limp, warm and relaxed. Feel the warmth and relaxation.

Now become aware of your heartbeat. Each time you exhale, mentally say, "My heartbeat is calm and regular." Imagine your heartbeat relaxed, calm, and regular.

Now place your hand on your upper abdomen. Each time you exhale, mentally say, "My abdomen (solar plexus) is warm." Imagine warmth flowing into your abdomen. Feel the warmth and relaxation.

Now just let your entire body be warm and relaxed, your mind calm and quiet. Let your breathing continue to be calm and regular, and enjoy the good, healthy sense of relaxation that now exists in your mind and body. While doing this, mentally say, "I am . . ." as you inhale and ". . . relaxed (calm)" as you exhale.

Now I'm going to count, slowly, from one to five. At the count of five, take a deep breath. On the inhale say, "Mind alert, wide awake," and open your eyes widely. On the exhale say, "Relaxed and refreshed." One. Coming up. Two. Three. Four. Five. Breathe in deeply. Say, "Mind alert, wide awake," and open your eyes. Exhale saying, "Relaxed and refreshed." Gently stretch all your muscles, then slowly get up, feeling alert and refreshed.

Controlled Breathing Exercises

Recently, respiratory control has come into use as a method for managing anxiety. Controlled breathing training assumes that hyperventilation, or overbreathing, is a problem which is caused by anxiety and further exacerbates anxiety. An increase in the rate of breathing causes one to expel too much carbon dioxide, resulting in alkalosis. A variety of uncomfortable sensations follow, such as dizziness, breathlessness, chest pain, sweating, and muscle spasms. (Shallow breathing is a normal stress response but becomes problematic when prolonged overbreathing occurs.) On overbreathing, Kennerley (1990, 26) writes: "A cycle of apprehension and overbreathing is set up, with the symptoms of hyperventilation augmenting the original fear, which may culminate in a panic attack."

Introducing controlled breathing involves first explaining why excessive breathing causes and increases anxiety, and then teaching controlled breathing methods. The relaxation training procedure which is detailed below is a variation of one developed by Clark et al. (1985) to help people control the symptoms of overbreathing.

Controlled breathing training teaches counselees a pattern of respiration that is incompatible with hyperventilation. They are taught to breathe calmly and regularly at a pace of eight to twelve breaths per minute, and are instructed to breathe from their diaphragm, not from their chest, inhaling through their nose. A transcript for controlled breathing follows.

> Let your eyelids be lightly closed or partially open. Adopt a let-it-happen, passive attitude and let relaxation occur at its own pace.
>
> Become aware of your body. Scan over it. Notice how it feels. Stay a passive observer of your environment but label whatever comes into your awareness. If it is a sound you hear, mentally say "sound." If it is a feeling, say "feeling." If it is a memory, say "memory." If it is a fantasy, say "fantasy." Do this for a while (a minute or so). /
>
> Now your breathing should be gentle and smooth. Put your right hand on your chest and your left hand on your stomach. Breathe through your nose using your diaphragm and not your chest. Allow your stomach to rise and fall gently with your breathing while your chest remains in place.
>
> Inhale, two, three, and four; Exhale, two, three, four, five, six, seven, and eight. Inhale, two, three, and four; Exhale, two, three, four, five, six, seven, and eight. Inhale, two, three, and four; Exhale, two, three, four, five, six, seven, and eight. Inhale, two, three, and four; Exhale, two, three, four, five, six, seven, and eight. Inhale, two, three, and four; Exhale, two, three, four, five, six, seven, and eight. (The helper slowly counts out loud the breathing pattern observing that the counselee appears comfortable. The pace of the breathing is decreased until it is 8-12 times per minute.)
>
> Continue breathing at this pace, mentally counting slowly to four on the inhale and eight on the exhale. Remember to use only

your diaphragm and breathe through your nose. Count your breaths for a while. (The helper is now quiet for about five minutes while the counselee practices controlled breathing. If the counselee appears to be experiencing problems, the exercise can be terminated early.)

Now just let your entire body be warm and relaxed, your mind calm and quiet. Let your breathing continue to be calm and regular, and enjoy the good, healthy sense of relaxation that now exists in your mind and body.

Now I'm going to count, slowly, from one to four. At the count of four, take a breath. On the inhale mentally say, "Mind alert, wide awake," and open your eyes. On the exhale say, "Relaxed and refreshed." One. Coming up. Two. Three. Four. Breathe in. Say, "Mind alert, wide awake," and open your eyes. Exhale saying, "Relaxed and refreshed." Gently stretch all your muscles, then slowly get up, feeling alert and refreshed.

Counselees at first may not feel as if they are getting enough air, but with practice they will find that they are able to slow the rate of their breathing and feel secure. If they find themselves panicking or lack confidence to control their breathing, they can breathe into a paper bag for a short period of time. (Instruct them to place the opening of the bag over their nose and mouth, and breathe as naturally as possible.) Counselees who have difficulty controlling their breathing sometimes find it helpful to totally expel all air from their lungs before beginning the exercise, after which they usually will be able to inhale more deeply.

A final method that helps some people to master controlled breathing is to lie down on their back with their right hand on the chest and their left hand on the stomach. Sometimes it is useful to actually push out the stomach while inhaling. This exercise helps the counselees better understand what correct breathing feels like, because it makes it easier for them to determine if they are breathing from the diaphragm (which is desirable) or from the chest (which is not).

RELAXATION METHODS IN BRIEF PASTORAL COUNSELING

Progressive relaxation, autogenic training, and controlled breathing can be used effectively in brief pastoral counseling. Following are some suggestions for enhancing that effectiveness:

The physical surroundings in which counselees practice relaxation training must be conducive to relaxation. The place

149

should be quiet and free of interruptions, illuminated with a low, gentle light. If outside noise (a pounding typewriter or ringing telephone, for example) is a problem, install a white-sound protector (available from companies that supply psychological therapeutic equipment) or simply turn on the fan in the heater or air conditioning unit and let it run continuously to provide a steady background hum. No office phone or intercom should ring. The temperature in the room needs to be made comfortable, possibly a degree or two warmer than usual. It is important, especially with autogenic training, that the person not be cold.

Individuals should be asked to wear loose-fitting clothing or loosen their garments a bit. Suggest that girdles and other tight garments not be worn during practice sessions. Occasionally counselees may wish to keep their eyes open until they are comfortable enough to close them. Those who wear contact lenses may want to remove them. People practicing relaxation should either sit or recline on a firm bed, couch, or comfortable chair. Many individuals seem to prefer a comfortable recliner for relaxation training.

Explain to counselees the purpose and benefits of relaxation training before the training is initiated. Explaining the possible benefits is important. If individuals do not understand or approve of the effort, if they fight the process, then it will not succeed.

Counselees will have to practice once or twice a day for about fifteen minutes until they learn to relax quickly. It is preferable that one session be in the morning, soon after they have awakened, and one in the evening. If trainees do not practice regularly they will not learn the skill. Part of the counseling covenant can include relaxation training and recording the results of each practice session.

A passive, let-it-happen attitude is required in order for people to relax. Tell trainees that they are learning a skill much like learning to drive a car, and that there is nothing magical to it. The difference between learning the skill and driving the car is that in learning this skill they are not to *try* in the way they usually learn a new skill; rather, they are to develop a passive attitude. They are to allow themselves to relax but not "force it" and not be upset if it doesn't happen right away. This is extremely important. "Not trying" can be upsetting to some people who fear losing control. I explain to trainees that they actually are in control: what is needed for relaxation is a passive self-control which allows the muscles to relax. For individuals familiar with spiritual direction and certain forms of contemplative or meditative prayer, these relaxation exercises can be interpreted as a preparation for such prayer.

Before beginning relaxation practice, a physical examination by the person's own doctor may be advised. If counselees have any doubts about their medical readiness, or in the case of progressive relaxation, if they are susceptible to muscle spasms or back, neck, or knee problems, a physician should definitely be consulted. Counselees using progressive relaxation methods need to be reminded not to tense their muscles too forcefully.

Some persons may feel odd physical sensations when first doing relaxation exercises, and it is good to let them know of that possibility. During the exercises some trainees will feel a floating sensation or a tingly or crawly feeling in fingers, arms, or legs. They may also feel uncomfortably warm. It is best to predict such possibilities before starting so that the people are not frightened by them if they occur.

At first, trainees use cassette tapes, but eventually they need to practice the exercises from memory. Frequently it is easier for counselees to practice relaxation if they begin by using a cassette tape of the exercise. Eventually counselees will need to be weaned from the tapes and practice at their own pace from memory. When they feel that the tape is moving too slowly, it is a sign that they do not need the tapes anymore. If, however, at any future time they should have difficulty in relaxing, then they can go back to the tapes. It is beneficial to use the complete tape once a month as a "booster shot" reinforcing the full relaxation method.

The minister's voice during practice sessions should be calm, slow, and relaxed. This means that the minister needs to be relaxed. Nothing is more fruitless than a tense pastor trying to train a tense counselee not to be tense. Failure is guaranteed. Ministers need to practice for themselves all the relaxation methods they plan to use before they administer them in counseling situations. Until these methods have been used for a while, the minister should probably practice along with the counselee. This helps to improve timing and to increase sensitivity throughout the process.

ADVANCED RELAXATION METHODS

The slow, step-by-step process described above seems necessary in the early stages of training while the person is learning to relax. Once the basic steps have been learned, however, more advanced methods may be used to generalize the learning, apply it more extensively to daily life, and shorten the time needed to achieve relaxation. A brief description of a few of the more helpful methods is included.

The full body progressive relaxation exercise. One advanced exercise, requiring only one or two minutes, is especially helpful to those who relax best with the progressive relaxation method. It involves simultaneously tensing as many muscles as one is capable of tensing. Counselees are instructed to stand on their tiptoes, clench their fists, scrunch up their faces, raise their shoulders, and tip their heads back. They are also to tighten as many other muscle groups as possible for five to seven seconds. This is followed by fifteen seconds of letting all muscles go limp and sensing the feeling of relaxation after releasing them. The method is best when used two or three times in succession.

Breathing exercise. A method that takes only a few minutes involves having the counselees close their eyes and monitor their breathing, focusing on the exhale. Then they are instructed to mentally say at each inhale, "I am" and at each exhale, "letting go."

In a variation on this method, counselees sit calmly, close their eyes, and focus on exhaling through the nose, repeating on each exhale the words "calm" or "relax." By continuing to do this, the pairing of relaxation with the words "calm" or "relax" is reinforced. In the future, the repetition of these words at tense moments in a busy day can bring relaxation.

Mini-vacation. In another exercise counselees use one of the three basic relaxation methods for a few minutes and then visualize a relaxing place or event, one that is calculated to calm rather than excite. For example, the minister may say: "See yourself floating on an inflatable raft on a quiet, sunny lake. Feel the warmth of the sun baking on your skin, the smell of the lake, the sound of the wind blowing through the pine trees on shore. Let your imagination go and allow all of your senses to become alive. Allow yourself to totally relax in this situation." This exercise provides a mini-vacation in the midst of a stressful day.

Meditation and the discipline of spiritual direction. Another mode of advanced relaxation training involves coupling any form of relaxation practice with meditative time or any of the classic disciplines of spiritual direction (Stone 1988). The two benefit each other.

Interventions other than relaxation training are useful for addressing anxiety in counselees (Kennerley 1990; Smith 1985). One of the benefits of relaxation training methods is that they can be used with relative ease in brief pastoral counseling. Many sessions of diagnosis and history-taking are not required before these methods can be applied, and the basics can be taught in the very first counseling session.

Relaxation, of course, is the opposite of anxiety. People who are anxious and come for counseling can be taught the skills of relaxation. These skills not only lessen anxiety-related physical ailments and improve interpersonal relationships, they also foster an openness and a patient waiting which is beneficial for hearing the Word spoken to us in our hectic lives.

Conclusion

Limits of Brief
Pastoral Counseling

An exciting opportunity came my way while I was in seminary. A psychiatrist from a renowned medical school invited selected students at local seminaries who were interested in pastoral care to attend a day-long session on mental health and the clergy, and I was among them.

My mood went from elation to disappointment to frustration, however, as the day wore on. The meeting began with an explanation of Freudian defense mechanisms, and progressed to a discussion of various types of psychopathology and the methods of treatment used by psychiatrists. The last hour of the day covered so-called warning signs of mental and emotional problems, and we future ministers were informed that because we were not equipped to handle emotional problems, persons we encountered who exhibited any of these warning signs should immediately be referred to a mental health professional.

I had hoped to learn more about counseling. I thought the workshop would expand our skills in offering pastoral care and counseling. Instead, the clear message was: "Ministers are not capable of handling these problems. What you are capable of doing is referring."

Recalling that seminar still brings a twinge of concern and irritation. Indeed, this same message is sometimes now handed out by specialists in pastoral counseling, albeit more subtly: parish ministers can do little more than refer, in this case to these new specialists. Is referral our only counseling task? Do ministers lack the necessary skills for helping people with their personal problems?

Many times referral is indeed a better option. Other times consulting with a mental health professional concerning a case is essential. But this book has made the point that ministers are capable of more than just recognizing warning signs. They are carers, counselors, and guides. They walk with people "through the darkest valley," through conflict and loss and despair, helping them to face crucial issues in their lives and guiding them with Christian sensitivities.

To be sure, some ministers see themselves as "little psychiatrists" instead of "little Christs" in their ministry, endeavoring to do everything that psychiatrists or psychologists do, although lacking the background of medical or psychological training to do so. To my mind such conduct is more than pretentious, it is unethical. In my experience, however, ministers more often do not place enough value on what they do and the skill they bring to the helping enterprise. They believe, like the message of that workshop I attended, that they are not capable of guiding people through difficult times. We need to work with our gifts and abilities as well as our limitations. Thousands of individuals every year are helped immeasurably by the pastoral counseling and care that ministers offer, mostly in less than the ten-session maximum for brief pastoral counseling used in this book.

In the day-to-day world, not the counseling book world where everyone gets better, brief pastoral counseling does not always bring the desired results. Many explanations can account for this. Some of the more crucial ones are:

■ The pastor is not the best helper for the individual.

■ The person does not want to change.

■ The person would be better assisted by a group within the church or a self-help group.

■ The person requires a form of help other than pastoral counseling (legal, medical, psychological testing, and so forth).

■ The counselee would benefit from longer counseling than the pastor's time and training allow.

Although some mental health professionals still insinuate that the only thing ministers should do is to recommend referral, I am more convinced than ever that ministers are able to offer quality care and counsel, far beyond merely recognizing warning signs. At the same time I am equally aware that we (myself included) have not

156

mastered many helping skills and sub-specialties of care. My abilities are better suited for some individuals than for others; certainly I am not able to help every person I encounter.

I also have learned that helping is more of a team effort than I first recognized. Pastoral care and counseling at its best is not performed by a "lone ranger" who puts on a white hat and gallops off to aid the needy individual. Frequently good pastoral care includes several helpers making certain that people get the care they require. The team may include psychologists, psychiatrists, medical, legal, and financial professionals, teachers, social workers, employers, and even the police.

For ministers, the task of caring is to some degree an administrative or organizational one. It includes structuring the situation so that the close friends of a bereaved person, for example, are there to help or so that an attorney or accountant in the congregation is consulted by a husband and wife who have overextended themselves financially.

REFERRAL

Ministers should counsel with the confidence that they possess skills and abilities that matter, but they also need to recognize their finitude and limitations. They must be willing to operate as team players, referring when needed, counseling when required, and knowing when to do what. Sometimes brief pastoral counseling is not effective because an individual needs the expertise of a special area of care; not to refer at such times is ethically precarious.

Ministers need to identify those times when they are not best suited for giving help. Any number of characteristics—personality, temperament, voice pattern, gender, age, political or social persuasion, heritage or background—may serve to build walls rather than clear paths. It is better to make a referral which has a chance of positive results than to spend a large amount of both minister's and parishioner's time on a fruitless effort.

There are two principal types of referral. In one, the minister surrenders the major responsibility for care to another professional. This type of referral is necessary in parish ministry in cases where persons are homicidal or suicidal, psychotic, or need hospitalization.

The other type of referral is also common in parish settings. In it, the minister retains primary responsibility for troubled persons' care, but sends them to specialists for particular kinds of help. For example, a parenting education center may be the referral source for a chaotic family with inadequate parenting skills, while the minister continues working with the couple on their marital difficulties.

Referral is a matter of timing, of taking into consideration both the counselees' mental and emotional states and the helper's own limitations. Time, skill, and emotional objectivity all play a role in determining when it is best to refer persons to more specialized care.

Time

Assuming that the pastoral carer has expertise to help in a troublesome situation, there is the question of whether she or he has enough time to handle it. It is important to answer quite frankly: Will I seriously neglect other responsibilities because of the time given to these individuals? Can I actually limit them to so many minutes or so many sessions per week? Will I be able to honestly and firmly limit my telephone availability? Will these limitations come at a cost to the healing process?

Skill

Even when time is sufficient, in some situations a caregiver's skills and experience may be less helpful than those of a specialist who has developed expertise in dealing with a particular problem. For example, few ministers or pastoral counselors are equipped to treat drug addiction effectively. Other situations that may call for specialized skills include evaluation and testing of children, financial debt counseling, chronic sexual dysfunction, and the like.

The caregiver needing to determine if he or she has the necessary skills to deal with a certain situation may ask the following questions: Do I feel comfortable working with this person? Can I be sure I am not misinterpreting this person's situation? Are we communicating clearly with one another, or are there frequent misunderstandings? After perhaps two or three sessions, is the person making changes? Am I fostering negative dependency?

As indicated above, any person who appears to be psychotic, violent, suicidal, or homicidal, or whose behavior is decidedly bizarre is a candidate for referral to another for primary care.

Emotional Objectivity

Even given adequate time and skills to deal with a particular situation, the caregiver's emotional objectivity needs to be examined.

Because of one's personal beliefs or values or past difficulties in resolving similar problems, some situations may elicit within the helper feelings of insecurity, hostility, threat, or anxiety. The caregiver must ask him- or herself the following questions: Is this a problem that I once faced but never successfully resolved? Do I need the counselee's personal approval to the degree that my authority and integrity are compromised? Am I becoming emotionally involved with the person or the situation? If the answer to any of these questions is yes, referral is in order.

When referral is needed, the following suggestions may apply:

■ When uncertain of where to refer, call a mental health professional in the congregation, a local crisis line, or an information and referral agency. Explain the situation and get up-to-date information on the appropriate person or agency. A direct call to the agency will reveal if they have a waiting list and if so how long, the fee schedule, and other pertinent information.

■ Not everyone will accept referral. Some may find that just considering referral is sufficient motivation to action. Others may only want to complain about their situation and not work toward a solution.

■ Referrals need to be made in a concrete way (not "I think you need to see a shrink" but "I'd be happy to recommend several marriage counselors; Dr. Feldman was helpful for my neighbors, and Dr. Terry has a very good reputation."

■ Suggest several referral sources, if possible, because one may be unavailable when it is needed.

■ If possible, the referral call is best made by the counselee. It may be helpful to suggest dialing the number immediately, or to offer a ride to the first appointment.

■ Remember that referral usually is not the first step in the care process, except in an emergency. It is important to establish a relationship, listen to the person's pain, and then gently move toward action, noting how the referral source can assist in the resolution of the problem.

■ After referring, follow-up is essential. One might telephone the next day to say "I called to find out how you are doing today, and to see if you had any problems scheduling a session with Dr. Feldman or Dr. Terry." If the person offers nothing but excuses, ask if there are other ways you can help, or if the individual wants to discuss things further. Mention that you will call again in a couple of days to see how they are doing. The helper should neither hound people nor let them get off too easily.

Referral to outside professionals is not a sign of defeat. Often it is inevitable. Even if one is a skillful pastoral carer, a healer, a guide, a reconciler and sustainer, it is a mark of competence to know when and how to refer.

WHEN NOTHING WILL HELP

Failure is hard to admit; wanting to keep trying more and more sessions and different methods is natural. Some helper or self-help group offers itself as the cure or hope. Indeed, some people will go from helper to helper believing that each new method or approach will finally cure their problem. Frequently, however, they are unwilling to pay the price for change or growth and may spend the rest of their lives seeking the elusive magic elixir.

While working at a suicide prevention center, I was astounded by the number of people who tried to upset or anger the helper so they could hang up the phone in a huff—presumably to prove to themselves that no one cared. It was a self-fulfilling prophecy. Occasionally people would go so far as to take their own lives because "no one cared." They didn't desire change.

A sufficient desire for help and change is needed, or little happens. So, when motivation is lacking in counselees, be patient enough to wait for the *kairos,* that critical moment when openness occurs and a new beginning can unfold. In such cases, releasing counselees so that they can experience the natural consequences of their decisions is better, in the hope that those consequences will create enough pain to make change and growth possible. Every individual is precious, yet with limited time and resources, hard ethical decisions must be made. One possible decision, perhaps the most loving one in the end, is to discharge those who are not working, to stop trying to help them.

Terminating is a hard decision to make. Here the person sits, perhaps crying, even begging for help, but if he or she is unwilling or unable to do the work required for change, then the minister is trapped by sympathy—not empathy—and this endangers the counselee's well-being. A sure guide is to *believe what they do, not what they say.* Continuing to offer unlimited support as their minister may put the minister in the role of what Alcoholics Anonymous calls an "enabler." Enablers make it easy for people to cling to their old, destructive patterns of behavior and indefinitely put off "hitting bottom"—that is, experiencing the amount of pain they need to motivate them to action.

How does the minister break the news of termination? How does the minister alter the relationship with counselees who are not ready for change? In brief, stating such news is not easy, particularly when the pastor relationship will continue after counseling. Distinguishing clearly between the counseling relationship and the care the minister gives the individual as part of the total ministry to the congregation is important. In those awkward, even tough situations, the pastor might say: "It appears to me you are not yet in enough pain to make the changes you say you want. . . ." A long pause may be necessary. Then the pastor goes on to say that it may be best to put aside the regular counseling sessions for the time being, stressing that he or she will continue to be there for them as their pastor and that at any time in the future, when they are more able or willing to take action, the counseling can be resumed.

Or, a more face-saving approach might be: "This seems to be a bad time for you take on these homework tasks. [Pause] After the holidays are over and your relatives have gone home [or your children are back in school, or you're settled in your new job, or school is out for the summer, and so forth], if this is something you would still like to address at that time, then we can schedule a few sessions and get some work done." Or, "Pain is the greatest motivator for change. Right now I don't believe you are in enough pain to make the effort to make change worthwhile. [Pause] You may get to that point later, maybe next week or maybe next year. Whenever you do, we can agree to work hard. In the meantime, I am still your pastor. There's a difference between pastoral counseling and the regular care that is a part of this congregation. Counseling involves a contract and calls for you to make specific changes and do homework tasks. Care is care. I will still care for you and be there for you."

As much as possible, make counselees feel like welcome guests. Stress the good things they are already doing and end by letting them know that the counseling can be started up again whenever they are ready.

One of the advantages of brief pastoral counseling is that counselees who do not really want to work often will simply quit early in the process. The short-term approach tests their level of commitment to change. When individuals are expected to be actively involved in counseling, do homework, and take active steps toward initiating change, those who prefer to complain often will remove themselves, and the pastor will not have to do a thing.

When releasing counselees who are active parishioners, they are neither out of sight nor out of mind. The pastor needs to wait, but with open eyes. When it appears that a real desire for growth is present, and a willingness to pay its price, the pastor initiates conversation (rather than waiting for them to do so) to renew the counseling process. For some people, however, such a moment may never occur.

CANDIDATES FOR BRIEF PASTORAL COUNSELING

Estimates vary about the percentage of people who would benefit from brief counseling. Some authors, such as Sifneos (1978) or Silver (1982), suggest that 20 percent of those seeing mental health professionals would profit from brief counseling methods. Others propose that brief counseling is best used with most counselees (Talmon 1990; Budman and Gurman 1988). What makes sense for the pastor, priest, rabbi, deacon, pastoral associate, or minister? With the increasing use and knowledge of specifically designed brief counseling approaches, practitioners increasingly view brief pastoral counseling as a viable method for greater numbers of persons.

Research on short-term counseling continues to mount and with it confidence in the brief approach as an appropriate and effective counseling method for a wide range of people. Brief counseling, by design rather than by default, is a field in its infancy. Much remains to be learned. All indications are that it is presently the superior primary approach for most parish ministers.

Some people clearly are *not* candidates for brief pastoral counseling. They include, for example, the following:

■ Individuals who appear to have a genetic, biological, chemical, or neurological problem (e.g., Alzheimer's disease, schizophrenia, and manic-depressive disorders).

■ Persons who need in-patient care (alcoholics requiring detoxification, drug addicts, and the seriously suicidal).

■ Those who want long-term care and are not willing or able to modify their expectations.

■ People who need to be under the primary care of a physician for medications or other medical reasons.

■ Individuals who have considerable difficulty establishing a relationship and are reticent to accept help.

Who is a candidate for brief pastoral counseling? Marmor (1979, 152) claims that the most important guideline for choosing candidates for brief counseling is "not diagnosis so much as the possession of certain personality attributes plus the existence of a focal conflict and a high degree of motivation." The foremost criterion for selecting brief pastoral counseling is not the presenting problem (for example, marital fighting, depression, lack of assertiveness) but the personal characteristics of the counselees. Budman and Gurman (1988) state that at present, no persuasive research exists to suggest that brief counseling is more beneficial for one type of problem than another. Rather, they assert, the person who does best in brief counseling is the same person who does well in any type of therapy, regardless of duration. Potentially successful counselees are:

■ Individuals who are able to come up with possible solutions to their present problem.

■ People who have successfully received help in the past.

■ People who can articulate a specific, concrete problem that is solvable.

■ Those who clearly have an unsolvable problem (such as the death of a child, a job layoff, a spouse who has left for someone else), but are willing to give up trying to change what is unchangeable and learn acceptance.

■ Persons who already have good support structures—church, family, friends—and are able to rely upon them.

■ Those who are highly motivated to bring about a change in their lives and are willing to devote time and energy to doing so.

■ Individuals experiencing an acute problem that they want to address, or a chronic one they are thoroughly weary of and want to change.

■ People who need only a listening ear (basic pastoral care supportiveness) who already know what they have to do and simply need to call upon someone who will listen.

■ Those who need referral, such as to an attorney, a financial advisor, a spiritual director, or a marriage counselor. Brief counseling calls for helping counselees get to those who can give them the help they need.

■ Those who would respond best to a group situation. Brief counseling can steer such people to a group that is suited to their needs—a prayer group, a self-help group such as Alcoholics Anonymous or Overeaters Anonymous, a cancer support group, or the like.

Likely candidates for brief pastoral counseling need have only some of these characteristics, although certainly the more exhibited, the better the chances for a successful resolution of the problem. The superior strategy for the minister (unless the person falls into one of the counter-indicated categories) is to begin using brief pastoral counseling. If this does not bear fruit, consider a switch either to long-term pastoral counseling or referral.

When brief pastoral counseling does not achieve its ends, it is not a sign of failure. Indeed, this may be the best diagnostic indicator for determining whether people are capable or willing to make changes in their lives.

Since the majority of all counseling is brief in nature, short-term pastoral counseling cannot be defined by the number of sessions alone, but rather by the *orientation* of the pastor toward the care being offered. Brief pastoral counseling has as much to do with the minister's attitude toward the helping process, and the specific interventions exercised, as it does with the number of sessions. Brief pastoral counseling employs whatever is the least invasive, simplest approach. It takes advantage of the "ripple effect" and assumes that a change initiated in one area of an individual's life generalizes and spreads to other areas. Most important is beginning the change process so that the success of change in one area can spread to others.

Brief pastoral counseling, then, is not so much a series of newly developed techniques as a broad outlook for counseling. It shapes how relationships are established, what questions are asked, how time is allotted, what therapeutic interventions are practiced and how they are applied. Brief pastoral counseling accepts our finitude. It accounts for the fact that we are part of a world caught up in individual and corporate sin, conflicts, losses, doubts, and anxieties. Evil is pervasive. Its task is not to eradicate all of these maladies because it cannot. Rather, it is to help those we serve to cope with the problems they face, and to be faithful to the call of God.

The viewpoint presented in this book has been that, for most people encountered in the parish, brief pastoral counseling methods are not only as good as longer methods—they actually are better in that they take less time to accomplish and are equally effective. For that reason they are the approach of first choice for clergy. Ministers do not need to be persuaded to offer brief counseling; like mental health professionals, they already are doing it. This book has attempted to address the inner conflict that arises when a minister believes in the superiority of long-term counseling but engages primarily in short-term care.

CONCLUSION

The likes of Woody Allen's "Max" may go to Lourdes or give counseling one more year, but they are the few. Brief pastoral counseling is a way to guide the many, in a reasonably short span of time, to address their problems, accept what must be accepted, and change what is possible to change. It helps people to make the changes that they need to make, and starts them on the path of growth and wholeness.

Appendix

This Pastoral Counseling Checklist was developed to enable ministers to quickly review the breadth of problems troubling individuals who have come to them for counseling. It is best administered in the initial session.

In brief pastoral counseling not all of the problem areas suggested by this checklist can be addressed. Rather, the data provide the helper with a background for the immediate problem the person has taken to counseling.

Items in the Pastoral Counseling Checklist are numbered under a single letter. The letter is an abbreviation for a category of problems, and all numbers that follow it are of the same category. For example, item #4, "I am troubled by my sin," is under R, indicating a problem of religious faith. The abbreviations are as follows:

R —Religious faith
I —Interpersonal and sexual difficulties
E —Emotional problems
P —Physical complaints
C —Job or career issues

It is helpful to scan the completed checklist to determine if most of the items checked are in one area or are evenly spread among all categories. If most are in one area, the minister can determine that the problem resides with that category (physical complaints, for example). If many items are checked and span all of the five categories, the individual is most likely under considerable stress which is expressing itself in a variety of ways in his or her life.

The author and publisher grant ministers the permission to duplicate this checklist, with proper citation, for use in their parish ministry.

167

Date _____/_____/_____

PASTORAL COUNSELING CHECKLIST
Howard Stone

NAME _____ PHONE _____

ADDRESS _____ AGE _____ SEX _____

Instructions: Carefully read each line. Check every item that applies to *you*.

R

- ☐ **1** My religious faith is not active enough in my life.
- ☐ **2** I am not close to anyone in the church.
- ☐ **3** Attending church doesn't help me.
- ☐ **4** I am troubled by my sin.
- ☐ **5** Prayer doesn't have much value for me.
- ☐ **6** I don't feel God's forgiveness of me.

R

- ☐ **7** I have little hope for the future.
- ☐ **8** I don't sense God's love for me.
- ☐ **9** I am concerned about my salvation.
- ☐ **10** I am losing my faith.
- ☐ **11** I need to confess and seek forgiveness for something.
- ☐ **12** I don't know what I want to do with my life.
- ☐ **13** I am the victim of racial or gender prejudice.
- ☐ **14** I have trouble with the opposite sex.
- ☐ **15** I am very shy.
- ☐ **16** I am uncomfortable with my sexual relations.

- ☐ **17** I have conflicts with my family.

I

- ☐ **18** I don't have anyone to talk to.
- ☐ **19** I have difficulty controlling my sex drives.
- ☐ **20** I can't talk about problems at home.
- ☐ **21** I am troubled by sexual attraction to those of my own sex.

P

- ☐ **22** I have many physical problems.
- ☐ **23** I have frequent headaches.
- ☐ **24** I have trouble sleeping.
- ☐ **25** I feel tired much of the time.
- ☐ **26** I have stomach problems (gas, ulcers, nervous stomach).
- ☐ **27** I drink and/or use drugs more than I would like.
- ☐ **28** I have menstrual or related problems.

E

- ☐ **29** I am unable to discipline myself.

- ☐ **30** I am frequently irritable.
- ☐ **31** I worry too much.
- ☐ **32** I often feel lonely.
- ☐ **33** I daydream a lot.
- ☐ **34** I feel life is not worth living.

E

- ☐ **35** I have little self-confidence.
- ☐ **36** I am often depressed or blue.
- ☐ **37** I find it hard to relax.
- ☐ **38** I am too much a perfectionist.
- ☐ **39** I have difficulty concentrating.

R

- ☐ **40** I do not feel the support of my fellow church members.
- ☐ **41** I have little or no meaning in life.
- ☐ **42** I am confused about my religious beliefs.
- ☐ **43** I want to feel closer to God.
- ☐ **44** I want to grow more spiritually.
- ☐ **45** I feel God is punishing me.

I

- ☐ **46** I am worried about my marriage.
- ☐ **47** I give in too easily to others.
- ☐ **48** I feel guilt over my sexual activities.
- ☐ **49** I think only of myself.
- ☐ **50** There is much complaining and/or quarrelling in my home.

I

- ☐ **51** A death of a family member or friend still troubles me.
- ☐ **52** I can be too dominating at times.
- ☐ **53** I am too inhibited in sex.
- ☐ **54** I am not getting along with some of my family.
- ☐ **55** I do not have enough recreation or social life.

I

- ☐ **56** It is hard for me to make friends.
- ☐ **57** I have difficulty getting along with others.
- ☐ **58** I miss friends and social life since moving here.
- ☐ **59** I am very sensitive about how others feel about me.
- ☐ **60** I need to be more assertive.

C

- ☐ **61** I wonder about a job or career change.
- ☐ **62** I am confused about what I want to do with my life.
- ☐ **63** I find little meaning in my work.
- ☐ **64** I have trouble managing my finances.
- ☐ **65** I am concerned about whether to return to work or school.

E

- ☐ **66** I procrastinate too much.
- ☐ **67** I am tense much of the time.
- ☐ **68** I entertain thoughts of suicide.
- ☐ **69** I have trouble controlling my temper.

☐ **70** I need to grow more personally.

☐ **71** I feel a failure.

E

☐ **72** I feel helpless and have difficulty coping.

☐ **73** I feel like giving up.

☐ **74** I am moody much of the time.

☐ **75** I am frequently angry.

☐ **76** I have a secret I'm afraid to tell others.

☐ **77** I take things too seriously.

Use the back of this sheet to describe your chief problems in your own words.

BRIEF PASTORAL COUNSELING
Fortress Press, 1994

Bibliography

Recommended readings on brief counseling for those working in parish ministry are identified with an asterisk (*).

Alberti, R. E., and M. L. Emmons. 1990. *Your Perfect Right*. San Luis Obispo, Calif.: Impact Press.

Bandler, R., and J. Grinder. 1979. *Frogs into Princes*. Moab, Utah: Real People Press.

————. 1982. *Reframing: Neuro-Linguistic Programming and the Transformation of Meaning*. Moab, Utah: Real People Press.

Barker, B. 1985. *Using Metaphors in Psychotherapy*. New York: Brunner/Mazel.

*Barry, W., and W. Connolly. 1983. *The Practice of Spiritual Direction*. New York: Seabury.

Beck, A. T. 1967. *Depression*. New York: Harper and Bros.

————. 1976. *Cognitive Therapy and the Emotional Disorders*. New York: International Universities Press.

————. 1979. *Cognitive Therapy of Depression*. New York: Thieme-Stratton.

*————. 1989. *Love Is Never Enough*. New York: Harper and Row.

Beck, D., and M. Jones. 1973. *Progress in Family Problems*. New York: Family Service Association of America.

*Benner, D. 1992. *Strategic Pastoral Counseling: A Short-Term Structure Model*. Grand Rapids, Mich.: Baker Book House.

Berenson, B. G., and K. M. Mitchell. 1974. *Confrontation!: For Better or Worse*. Amherst: Human Resource Development Press.

Berg, I. 1991. "Working with the Problem Drinker: A Solution-Focused Approach," Lecture, American Association of Marriage and Family Therapists national convention. Dallas.

Berg, I., and S. Miller. 1992. *Working with The Problem Drinker: A Solution-Focused Approach*. New York: W. W. Norton.

Bergman, J. 1985. *Fishing for Barracuda: Pragmatics of Brief Systemic Therapy*. London: W. W. Norton.

Budman, S., and A. Gurman. 1988. *Theory and Practice of Brief Therapy*. New York: Guilford Press.

Burns, D. 1980. *Feeling Good*. New York: Signet Books.

Burns, D., and A. Beck. 1978. "Cognitive Behavior Modification of Mood Disorders." In *Cognitive Behavior Therapy: Research and Application*. Edited by J. Foreyt and D. Rathjen, 109–34. New York: Plenum Press.

Cade, B., and W. O'Hanlon. 1993. *A Brief Guide to Brief Therapy*. New York: W. W. Norton.

★Capps, D. 1990. *Reframing: A New Method in Pastoral Care*. Minneapolis: Fortress Press.

———. 1993. *The Depleted Self: Sin in a Narcissistic Age*. Minneapolis: Fortress Press.

★Childs, B. 1990. *Short-Term Pastoral Counseling*. Nashville: Abingdon Press.

Clark, D. M., P. M. Salkovskis, and A. J. Chalkley. 1985. "Respiratory Control as a Treatment for Panic Attacks." *Journal of Behavioral Therapy and Experimental Psychiatry* 16:23–30.

★Clinebell, H. 1977. *Basic Types of Pastoral Care and Counseling*. Nashville: Abingdon Press. 2d ed., 1984.

Cox, R. 1972. "Short-Term Counseling Techniques." *Journal of Pastoral Care* 26:166–71.

★de Shazer, S. 1985. *Keys to Solution in Brief Therapy*. New York: W. W. Norton.

———. 1988. *Clues: Investigating Solutions in Brief Therapy*. New York: W. W. Norton.

———. 1991. *Putting Difference to Work*. New York: W. W. Norton.

Driscoll, R. 1984. *Pragmatic Psychotherapy*. New York: Van Nostrand Reinhold.

★Egan, G. 1993. *The Skilled Helper*. 5th ed. Pacific Grove, Calif.: Brooks/Cole Publishing Company.

Ellis, A. A., and R. A. Harper. 1975. *A New Guide to Rational Living*. Los Angeles: Wilshire Book Co.

Erickson, M. 1980. *Innovative Psychotherapy*. Vol. 4 of *Collected Papers*. Edited by E. Rossi. New York: Irvington.

Fairchild, R. 1980. *Finding Hope Again: A Pastor's Guide to Counseling Depressed Persons*. New York: Harper & Row.

Fisher, S. 1980. "The Use of Time Limits in Brief Psychotherapy: A Comparison of Six-Session, Twelve-Session, and Unlimited Treatment with Families." *Family Process* 19:377–92.

———. 1984. "Time-Limited Brief Therapy with Families: A One-Year Follow-up Study." *Family Process* 23:101–6.

Frank, J. 1979. "The Present Status of Outcome Studies." *Journal of Consulting and Clinical Psychology* 47:310–16.

Furman, B., and T. Ahola. 1992. *Solution Talk: Hosting Therapeutic Conversations*. New York: W. W. Norton.

Garetz, F., R. Kogl, and D. Wiener. 1959. "A Comparison of Random and Judgmental Methods of Determining Mode of Outpatient Mental Hygiene Treatment." *Journal of Clinical Psychology* 15:401–2.

Garfield, S. 1980. *Psychotherapy: An Eclectic View.* New York: Wiley.

Garfield, S., and R. Kurtz. 1977. "A Study of Eclectic Views." *Journal of Consulting and Clinical Psychology* 45:78–83.

Goffman, E. 1974. *Frame Analysis.* Rockville: Aspen.

Goldfried, M. R. 1971. "Systematic Desensitization as Training in Self-Control." *Journal of Consulting and Clinical Psychology* 36:228–34.

Goldfried, M. R., and G. C. Davison. 1976. *Clinical Behavior Therapy.* New York: Holt, Rinehart, and Wilson.

Gordon, T. 1970. *Parent Effectiveness Training.* New York: Peter H. Wyden.

Haley, J. 1963. *Strategies of Psychotherapy.* New York: Grune and Stratton.

————. 1973. *Uncommon Therapy: The Psychiatric Techniques of Milton H. Erickson, M.D.* New York: W. W. Norton.

————. 1976. *Problem-Solving Therapy: New Strategies for Effective Family Therapy.* San Francisco: Jossey-Bass.

————. 1985. *Conversations with Milton H. Erickson, M. D.* New York: Triangle Press.

*Hauck, P. A. 1972. *Reason in Pastoral Counseling.* Philadelphia: Westminster Press.

————. 1973. *Overcoming Depression.* Philadelphia: Westminster Press.

————. 1974. *Overcoming Frustration and Anger.* Philadelphia: Westminster Press.

————. 1975. *Overcoming Worry and Fear.* Philadelphia: Westminster Press.

*————. 1980. *Brief Counseling with RET.* Philadelphia: Westminster Press.

Jacobson, E. 1974. *Progressive Relaxation.* 3d ed. Chicago: University of Chicago Press.

Janis, I., and I. Lester. 1983. *Short-Term Counseling: Guidelines Based on Recent Research.* New Haven: Yale University Press.

Johnson, D., and C. Gelso. 1980. "The Effectiveness of Time Limits in Counseling and Psychotherapy." *The Counseling Psychologist* 9:70–82.

Kanfer, F. H., and A. P. Goldstein, eds. 1980. *Helping People Change: A Textbook of Methods.* 2d ed. Vol. 52. Pergamon General Psychology Series. New York: Pergamon Press.

Kanfer, F. H., and B. K. Schefft. 1988. *Guiding the Process of Therapeutic Change.* Champaign, Ill.: Research Press.

Kennerley, N. 1990. *Managing Anxiety: A Training Manual.* London: Oxford University Press.

Langsley, D. 1978. "Comparing Clinic and Private Practice of Psychiatry." *American Journal of Psychiatry* 135:702–6.

Langsley, D., P. Machotka, and K. Flomenhaft. 1971. "Avoiding Mental Hospital Admission: A Follow-up Study." *American Journal of Psychiatry* 132:177–79.

*Lazarus, A. 1977. *In the Mind's Eye.* New York: Guilford Press.

Leventhal, T., and G. Weinberger. 1975. "Evaluation of a Large-Scale Brief Therapy Program for Children." *American Journal of Orthopsychiatry* 49:119–33.

Liberman, B. L. 1978. "The Role of Mastery in Psychotherapy: Maintenance of Improvement and Prescriptive Change." In *Effective Ingredients of Successful Psychotherapy*. Edited by J. D. Frank, R. Hoehn-Saric, S. D. Imber, B. L. Liberman, and A. R. Stone. New York: Brunner/Mazel.

Luborsky, L., and B. Singer. 1975. "Comparative Studies of Psychotherapies." *Archives of General Psychiatry* 32:995–1008.

Mandel, H. 1981. *Short-Term Psychotherapy and Brief Treatment Techniques: An Annotated Bibliography, 1920–1980*. London: Plenum Press.

Mann, J. 1973. *Time-Limited Psychotherapy*. Cambridge, Mass.: Harvard University Press.

Mann, J., and R. Goldman. 1982. *A Casebook in Time-Limited Psychotherapy*. New York: McGraw-Hill.

Marmor, J. 1979. "Short-Term Dynamic Psychotherapy." *American Journal of Psychiatry* 136:2, Feb. 1979, 149–55.

Meltzoff, J., and M. Kornreich. 1970. *Research in Psychotherapy*. New York: Atherton Press.

Minuchin, S. 1988. *Psychosomatic Families: Anorexia Nervosa in Context*. Cambridge, Mass.: Harvard University Press.

Munro, A., B. Manthei, and J. Small. 1989. *Counseling: The Skills of Problem-Solving*. London: Routledge.

Nouwen, H. 1979. *The Wounded Healer*. Garden City, N.J.: Doubleday.

O'Hanlon, W. 1987. *Taproots: Underlying Principles of Milton Erickson's Therapy and Hypnosis*. New York: W. W. Norton.

*O'Hanlon, W., and M. Weiner-Davis. 1989. *In Search of Solutions*. New York: W. W. Norton.

Papp, P. 1980. "The Greek Chorus and Other Techniques of Paradoxical Therapy." *Family Process* 19:45–57.

*Paterson, G. R. 1974. *Families*. Champaign, Ill.: Research Press.

Phillips, E. L. 1985. *A Guide for Therapists and Patients to Short-Term Psychology*. Springfield, Ill.: Charles C. Thomas.

Phillips, E. L., and D. Weiner. 1962. *Discipline, Achievement and Mental Health*. Englewood Cliffs, N.J.: Prentice-Hall.

———. 1966. *Short-Term Psychotherapy and Structured Behavior Change*. New York: McGraw-Hill.

Rathus, S., and J. Nevid. 1977. *Behavioral Therapy: Behavioral Therapy Strategies for Solving Problems in Living*. Garden City, N.Y.: Doubleday.

Reid, W., and A. Shyne. 1969. *Brief and Extended Casework*. New York: Columbia University Press.

Rosen, S., ed. 1982. *My Voice Will Go with You: The Teaching Tales of Milton H. Erickson*. New York: W. W. Norton.

Rossi, E., M. Ryan, and F. Sharp. 1983. *Healing in Hypnosis: The Seminars, Workshops, and Lectures of Milton H. Erickson, Volume 1*. New York: Irvington Press.

Samuels, M., and N. Samuels. 1975. *Seeing with the Mind's Eye*. New York: Bookworks.

Schultz, J. H., and W. Luthe. 1959. *Autogenic Training*. New York: Grune & Stratton.

Seltzer, L. 1986. *Paradoxical Strategies in Psychotherapy: A Comprehensive Overview and Guidebook*. Chichester, England: John Wiley and Sons.

Shelton, J. L., and R. L. Levy. 1981. *Behavioral Assignments and Treatment Compliance: Handbook of Clinical Strategies*. Champaign, Ill.: Research Press.

Sifneos, P. 1972. *Short-Term Psychotherapy and Emotional Crisis*. Cambridge, Mass.: Harvard University Press.

————. 1978. "Evaluation Criteria for Selection of Patients." In *Basic Principles and Techniques in Short-Term Dynamic Psychotherapy*. Edited by H. Davanloo, 433–53. New York: Spectrum.

Silver, R. 1982. "Brief Dynamic Psychotherapy: A Critical Look at the State of the Art." *Psychiatric Quarterly* 53:275–82.

Sloane, R., F. Staples, A. Cristol, N. Yorkston, and K. Whipple. 1975. *Psychotherapy Versus Behavior Therapy*. Cambridge, Mass.: Harvard University Press.

★Smith, J. C. 1985. *Relaxation Dynamics: Nine World Approaches to Self-Relaxation*. Champaign, Ill.: Research Press.

Steiper, D., and D. Weiner. 1959. "The Problem of Interminability in Outpatient Psychotherapy." *Journal of Consulting Psychology* 23:237–42.

Stone, H. 1988. *The Word of God and Pastoral Care*. Nashville: Abingdon Press.

————. 1991. *The Caring Church: A Guide for Lay Pastoral Care*. 2d ed., rev. Minneapolis: Fortress Press.

————. 1993. *Crisis Counseling*. 2d ed., rev. Minneapolis: Fortress Press.

Stone, H., and W. Clements. 1991. *Handbook for Basic Types of Pastoral Care and Counseling*. Nashville: Abingdon Press.

Strupp, H. 1978. "Psychotherapy Research and Practice: An Overview." In *Handbook of Psychotherapy and Behavior Change*, 2nd ed., edited by S. Garfield and A. Bergin, 3–22. New York: Wiley.

★Talmon, M. 1990. *Single-Session Therapy: Maximizing the Effect of the First (and Often Only) Therapeutic Encounter*. San Francisco: Jossey-Bass.

Thurneysen, E. 1962. *A Theology of Pastoral Care*. Richmond, Va.: John Knox Press.

★Underwood, R. 1985. *Empathy and Confrontation in Pastoral Care*. Philadelphia: Fortress Press.

Walen, S. R., R. DeGuiseppe, and R. L. Wessler. 1980. *A Practitioner's Guide to Rational-Emotive Therapy*. New York: Oxford University Press.

Watzlawick, P. 1978. *The Language of Change: Elements of Therapeutic Communication*. New York: Basic Books.

Watzlawick, P., J. H. Weakland, and R. Fisch. 1974. *Change: Principles of Problem Formation and Problem Resolution*. New York: W. W. Norton.

Weakland, J., R. Fisch, P. Watzlawick, and A. Bodin. 1974. "Brief Therapy: Focused Problem Resolution." *Family Therapy Networker* 13:141–68.

Wells, R. 1977. "Communication Training vs. Conjoint Marital Therapy." *Social Work Research and Abstracts* 13: 31–39.

————. 1982. *Planned Short-Term Treatment.* New York: The Free Press.

Wolberg, L. R. 1980. *Handbook of Short-Term Psychotherapy.* New York: Thieme-Stratton.

Wolpe, J. 1964. "The Systematic Desensitization Treatment of Neuroses." In *Experiments in Behavior Therapy,* edited by H. J. Eysenck, 21–39. Oxford: Pergamon Press.

Zeig, J. 1980. *A Teaching Seminar with Milton H. Erickson, M.D.* New York: Brunner/Mazel.

Ziboorg, G., and G. W. Henry. 1941. *A History of Medical Psychology.* New York: W. W. Norton.